NATIONAL CLIMATE CHANGE STRATEGY IRELAND

October 2000

BAILE ÁTHA CLIATH

ARNA FHOILSIÚ AG OIFIG AN tSOLÁTHAIR

Le ceannach díreach ón

OIFIG DHÍOLTA FOILSEACHÁN RIALTAS,

TEACH SUN ALLIANCE, SRÁID THEACH LAIGHEAN, BAILE ÁTHA CLIATH 2,

nó tríd an bpost ó

FOILSEACHÁN RIALTAS, AN RANNÓG POST-TRÁCHTA,

4-5 BÓTHAR FHEARCHAIR, BAILE ÁTHA CLIATH 2,

(Teil: 01 661 3111 - fó-line 4040/4045; Fax 01 475 2760)

nó trí aon díoltóir leabhar.

DUBLIN

PUBLISHED BY THE STATIONERY OFFICE

To be purchased directly from the

GOVERNMENT PUBLICATIONS SALE OFFICE,

SUN ALLIANCE HOUSE, MOLESWORTH STREET, DUBLIN 2,

or by mail order from,

GOVERNMENT PUBLICATIONS, POSTAL TRADE SECTION,

4 - 5 HARCOURT ROAD, DUBLIN 2

(Tel: 01 661 3111 - ext. 4040/4045; Fax 01 475 2760)

or through any bookseller

PN no. 9114   ISBN No: 0707665892

£10.00

NATIONAL CLIMATE CHANGE STRATEGY

Contents

MINISTER'S FOREWORD

In recent years, extreme weather events around the world have focused our minds on the potentially devastating impacts of climate change. Scientists have concluded that human activity is now influencing the global climate. Ireland could experience higher winter rainfall with more severe flooding, lower summer rainfall and water shortages, rising sea levels, accelerated coastal erosion, loss of bogland, and threats to agriculture due to additional pests and diseases.

We are living with the consequences of actions and decisions over the last 100 to 200 years, and future generations must live with the consequences of ours. Addressing climate change now is our responsibility. The developed world has made a start, agreeing under the Kyoto Protocol to cut greenhouse gas emissions by some 5% by the end of the decade, but recognising that much more substantial cuts must be made over the course of the century. We are working with our EU partners to ratify the Protocol by 2002, and the Government is embarking on a challenging programme to limit the growth in emissions in the short to medium term, so that we can increase our ambition into the future.

Some climate change impacts are already unavoidable. Averting the worst effects means acting now to place global and national development on a more sustainable path.

Business as usual is no longer an option for Ireland. Our record economic growth means that, even with flexibility to complete our development against a low baseline in 1990, our strategy must be radically different in the coming decade. We have already reached our Kyoto 13% growth limitation target. Now, we have to achieve the difficult task of dramatically reducing greenhouse gas emissions over this decade. We intend to do so in a manner that protects our economy, that is equitable, and that will place a premium on efficiency and on technical innovation.

This Strategy provides a framework for the radical action that is necessary to meet Ireland's climate change commitment.

Key initiatives will include: -

▶ Carbon energy taxation,

▶ Use of emissions trading,

▶ Measures supportive of ending coal-firing at Moneypoint,

▶ Fuel switching to low and zero carbon fuels,

▶ Livestock reductions and lower fertiliser use,

▶ Fuel efficiency, demand management and modal shift in transport,

▶ Energy efficiency in construction,

▶ Adjustment of the new house grant.

We need to make changes right across the economy and society: to the way we work and in attitudes and awareness. This Strategy will now place that process firmly on track, with fundamental and large-scale changes, and with smaller actions which also illustrate how easy it is to make a difference.

In partnership with EU Member States and the wider international community, and more particularly, with economic sectors and the Irish public, the Government is determined that we will successfully tackle climate change for the benefit of present and future generations.

Noel. Dempsey

EXECUTIVE SUMMARY

International Context

Climate change is identified as the most significant and threatening global environmental problem facing humanity today. Global consensus has recognised that cuts of up to 70% in global emissions are needed over the next century in order to stabilise concentrations in the atmosphere at twice the pre-industrial level. The impacts of climate change on Ireland will be significant, but will be more damaging on many countries which are least able to afford to take action or adapt.

As a first step towards tackling this threat, the United Nations Framework Convention on Climate Change (UNFCCC) required developed countries to put in place policies and measures with the objective of returning emissions of greenhouse gases to 1990 levels by the end of the decade. However, in recognition of the need to take more substantial action, developed countries agreed legally binding targets in Kyoto in 1997, to reduce global emissions of six greenhouse gases by 5.2% in the period from 1990 to 2012. The EU will reduce emissions by 8% overall.

Irish Target

As part of the EU target, Ireland has agreed to limit the growth in greenhouse gas emissions by 13% above 1990 levels. Without the action set out in this Strategy, it is projected that net annual emissions would increase by 37.3%. Reductions of emissions of 13.1 million tonnes (Mt) CO_2 equivalent on this projected figure will be required to meet the national target.

Sources of Irish Emissions

The main greenhouse gas in Ireland is carbon dioxide (CO_2), mainly arising from the burning of fossil fuel in transport, heating and electricity generation. Irish emissions of other greenhouse gases, including methane (CH_4) and nitrous oxide (N_2O) are proportionately higher than other countries, and emissions from the agriculture sector were 35% of all greenhouse gas emissions in 1990, the highest of all sectors. Emissions from the transport sector are forecast to have the largest increase (by 180%) by 2010.

Strategic Framework for Action

This Strategy provides a framework for achieving greenhouse gas emissions reductions in the most efficient and equitable manner while continuing to support economic growth and to prepare Ireland for the more ambitious commitments that will be required after 2012. It requires action to be taken in all sectors, as early as possible and in a sustainable manner. The Strategy is based on the fundamental principles of sustainable development which are set out in *Sustainable Development: A Strategy for Ireland*, and takes account of the need to protect economic development and competitiveness.

Guiding Principles

The Strategy recognises that the burden for the Kyoto commitment period and beyond must be borne equitably within the economy. The criteria to achieve this include: -

▸ the requirement to promote sustainable development,

▸ maximisation of economic efficiency, including a preference for the use of "no regret" and least cost measures,

▸ achievement of sectoral equity (relative costs and effort, achievement of reductions across the economy),

▸ protection of economic development and competitiveness (market based instruments, exploitation of new markets and opportunities),

▸ generating an impetus for early action.

Reductions of emissions will be achieved through an integrated approach, using the full range of instruments and policy options. These include: -

▸ the use of economic instruments (including taxation and emissions trading) with broad sectoral and/or cross-sectoral application,

▸ a broad range of policies and measures tailored specifically to relevant sectors,

▸ a vigorous and appropriate pursuit of common and coordinated policies and measures implemented at EU and wider international levels, and,

▸ participation in international emissions trading.

Summary of the measures

The key measures in the Strategy are: -

cross-sectoral market based instruments, including: -

▶ **taxation** – Appropriate tax measures, prioritising CO_2 emissions, will be introduced from 2002 on a phased, incremental basis across a broad range of sectors in a manner that takes account of national economic, social and environmental objectives.

▶ Ireland will participate in the pilot EU **emissions trading** scheme and in **international emissions trading.**

In the **energy** sector: -

▶ Measures supportive of ceasing of coal use at Moneypoint by 2008 and fuel switching towards less carbon intensive fuels.

▶ An expansion of renewable energy.

▶ Maximisation of CHP.

▶ An enhanced demand side management programme under the Irish Energy Centre.

In the **transport** sector: -

▶ Fuel Efficiency Measures
  ▶ further rebalancing of VRT and annual motor tax to favour more fuel-efficient cars,
  ▶ fuel economy labelling for all new cars,
  ▶ fuel switching and efficiency for the public transport and State vehicles.

▶ Modal Shift Measures
  ▶ increased use of public transport through additional investment in public transport to improve existing suburban bus and rail facilities and to develop new facilities.

▶ Demand Management
  ▶ setting fuel taxes at appropriate levels to limit the rate of increase in overall fuel consumption and to progressively reduce the incentive for purchase of fuel for foreign vehicles in the State,
  ▶ development of integrated traffic management,
  ▶ achieving higher residential densities; restrictions on out of town retail units.

In the **industrial, commercial and services** sector: -

▶ Market instruments, including targeted taxation measures and emissions trading.

▶ Negotiated agreements with industry, with the option for firms complying with agreements to reduce their tax burden.

▶ The examination of investment support from the perspective of greenhouse gas emissions.

▶ Expansion of Irish Energy Centre programmes.

▶ Specific measures to tackle industrial gases e.g. agreement on the use of alternatives.

In the **agriculture** sector: -

▶ A reduction in CH_4 from the national herd, equivalent to a reduction in livestock numbers by 10% below 2010 projected levels; an appropriate balance will be maintained between direct reductions in stock numbers and intensification of other measures, including a prioritised research programme (including feeding programmes, additives, probiotics, engineering and finishing cattle at a younger age) to identify means of reducing emissions per animal.

▶ Strengthened relationship between agriculture and forestry policy in REPS, to promote additional forestry plantation at farm level.

▶ Development of short-rotation biomass and anaerobic digestion of animal wastes for energy generation.

▶ Use of nitrogenous fertiliser will be reduced by 10% below expected 2010 levels, supplemented by other measures (including use of slow release inhibitors, efficient management of slurry and dirty water) to reduce N_2O emissions from soils.

▶ Best practice guidelines will be developed to encourage changing farming practices.

In the **forestry** sector, measures to enhance carbon sinks will be supported by: -

▶ Review of the forestry programme to ensure full achievement of planting target and the intensification of the programme.

▶ Research programme to maximise sequestration potential of forestry.

In the **built environment and residential** sector: -

▸ Improved spatial and energy use planning – (Residential Density Guidelines, the National Spatial Strategy, Strategic Planning Guidelines).

▸ More efficient new buildings – Building Regulations will be reviewed to reduce energy use in new housing by up to 20% in 2002 with further reductions in 2005.

▸ Sustainable building will be encouraged through adjustment of the New House Grant to require that standards of energy efficiency are met, and support for low energy projects in all categories of housing.

▸ Improved efficiency of existing building through education and awareness programmes to promote domestic energy efficiency, changing the fuel mix in households, energy efficiency rating for housing.

▸ For pre-1991 building stock, energy rating will be introduced; in the case of local authority housing, schemes to upgrade the stock will address energy efficiency and have a focus on alleviating fuel poverty where appropriate.

Local Authorities are identified as having an important cross-sectoral role at local level, including in partnership with Local Energy Agencies. Local authorities will be encouraged to adopt best international practice as developed through international networks, and will develop appropriate performance indicators of their progress in reducing emissions. Measures in the **waste sector** will be in accordance with the national policy framework set out in *Changing Our Ways*. Waste generators will pay the full cost of waste collection, treatment and disposal, including the development of charges for household and commercial waste. The implementation of Waste Management Plans by local authorities will be vigorously pursued.

Implementation of Strategy

Government and relevant State Agencies will immediately undertake the necessary work to implement the measures, overseen by a high level inter-Departmental group. Comhar has been asked to support implementation by identifying means of securing necessary changes in behaviour. Progress will be assessed regularly by the Minister for the Environment and Local Government, and the Strategy will be subject to biennial review.

Quantified Indicative Reductions Proposed in Strategy

ENERGY

Fuel Switching to Gas	4.15 Mt CO_2
Moneypoint	*3.4 Mt CO_2*
Oil	*0.75 Mt CO_2*
CHP	0.25 Mt CO_2
Renewables	1.0 Mt CO_2
Efficiencies	0.1 Mt CO_2
DSM	0.15 Mt CO_2
Total	**5.65 Mt CO_2**

TRANSPORT

Vehicle Efficiency Improvements	0.77 Mt CO_2
Fuel Measures (displace bunkering)	0.9 Mt CO_2
VRT, Taxes	0.5 Mt CO_2
Labelling	0.1 Mt CO_2
Public Transport Measures	0.15 Mt CO_2
Traffic Management	0.2 Mt CO_2
Freight	0.05 Mt CO_2
Total	**2.67 Mt CO_2**

BUILT ENVIRONMENT & RESIDENTIAL

Building Regulation Standards	0.25 Mt CO_2
Existing Buildings	0.4 Mt CO_2
Fuel Mix	0.25 Mt CO_2
Total	**0.9 Mt CO_2**

INDUSTRY, COMMERCIAL, SERVICES

"No regrets"/low cost energy efficiency gains	0.75 Mt CO_2
Up to £75 tonne CO_2 efficiency measures	0.25 Mt CO_2
Process Substitution for Cement	0.5 Mt CO_2
Industrial Gases	0.5 Mt CO_2 equivalent
Commercial and Services	0.175 Mt CO_2
Total	**2.175 Mt CO_2 equivalent**

AGRICULTURE

Reduction of CH_4 from national herd	1.2 Mt CO_2 equivalent
of which Feeding Regimes	*0.5 Mt CO_2 equivalent*
Fertiliser Use	0.9 Mt CO_2 equivalent
On-Farm Forestry Sequestration	0.25 Mt CO_2
Manure Management	0.06 Mt CO_2 equivalent
Total	**2.41 Mt CO_2 equivalent**

SINKS (Additional Sequestration)	**0.76 Mt CO_2 equivalent**
WASTE	**0.85 Mt CO_2 equivalent**
OVERALL TOTAL	**15.415 Mt CO_2 equivalent**

6

GLOSSARY OF TERMS

Adaptation
(to climate change) is the taking of measures to cope with the effects of climate change, rather than the action taken to reduce emissions.

Anaerobic decomposition/ digestion
The breakdown of organic materials in the absence of air (oxygen). CH_4 is a by-product, either vented to the atmosphere or used as an energy source

Anthropogenic
Human induced; as a result of human actions.

Base year
The year against which commitments under the Kyoto Protocol are measured. Emissions levels in 1990 set the basis for determining the national limitation target of 13% (a base year of 1995 will be used for the industrial gases).

BAT
Best Available Techniques under the EU Integrated Pollution Prevention and Control (IPPC) Directive (96/61/EC).

bn
Billion.

CAP
Common Agricultural Policy (of the EU).

CCGT
Combined Cycle Gas Turbine (for electricity generation). Electricity is generated from both the gas turbine (akin to a jet engine) and from the waste heat.

CDM
Clean Development Mechanism (see end of Chapter 2).

CFCs
Chlorofluorocarbons. A family of ozone depleting substances whose use is banned for most purposes under the Montreal Protocol on Substances that Deplete the Ozone Layer (1987). While CFCs are also greenhouse gases, they are excluded from the UNFCCC and Kyoto Protocol as their use is controlled under the Montreal Protocol.

CH_4
Methane. The second most significant greenhouse gas. Naturally occurring and also arising from human activity.

CHP
Combined Heat and Power. The waste heat from electricity generation is put to another useful purpose.

Climate change
The global climate system is subject to natural variation. In the context of this Strategy, the UNFCCC and Kyoto Protocol, what is meant is that change in climate attributable to human activity arising from the release of greenhouse gases into the atmosphere and which is additional to natural climate variability.

CO_2
Carbon Dioxide. The main greenhouse gas arising from human activities, and also naturally occurring. Atmospheric concentrations have risen from about 280ppm prior to the industrial revolution to about 340ppm now.

CO_2 efficient
(generally fuels). Those that release less CO_2 per unit of energy generated than others. Natural gas is more "CO_2 efficient" than coal, as carbon is a lesser constituent of natural gas and less CO_2 is released than in the combustion of coal to produce the same energy output.

CO_2 equivalent
Where gases other than CO_2 are referred to, for comparison purposes these are converted to their equivalence in global warming terms to CO_2. See GWP. Sequestration rates of carbon are quantified in terms of CO_2 removed from the atmosphere.

COFORD
National Council for Forest Research and Development, Agriculture Building, UCD, Belfield, Dublin 4.
Phone (01) 7067700,
fax (01) 7061180,
website: http://www.coford.ie/

Comhar
National Sustainable Development Partnership. Comhar's terms of reference are to advance the national agenda for sustainable development, to evaluate progress in this regard, to assist in devising suitable mechanisms and advising on their implementation, and to contribute to the formation of a national consensus in these regards.

Commitment period
The Kyoto Protocol provides that Parties' targets are to be achieved over the 5-year period 2008 – 2012 (the "first commitment period"). Targets for future commitment periods (post 2012) are yet to be negotiated.

Common and coordinated policies and measures
(in an EU Context). *Common* policies are those requiring common action across all member states, usually on foot of an initiative by the European Commission. *Coordinated* policies and measures are those where common action is not required, but where benefits accrue through member states taking action on a joint basis.

COP, COP6
Conference Of the Parties (to the UNFCCC). This meets annually; the 6th Conference (COP6) is to meet in The Hague in November 2000.

Cross-sectoral
Pertaining to more than one, or many, sectors of the economy.

DSM
Demand Side Management. In the energy sector, the management and reduction of energy use through incentives and other measures to reduce and/or manage more efficiently customer demand for energy.

DTI
Dublin Transportation Initiative.

DTO
Dublin Transportation Office.

Environmental Network of Government Departments
The Inter-Departmental Committee at senior official level concerned with advancing environmental integration. It is chaired by the Department of the Environment and Local Government

EMAS	Eco-Management and Audit Scheme under Council Regulation (EEC) No. 1836/93 allowing voluntary participation by companies in the industrial sector in a Community eco-management and audit scheme. (Review of Regulation being finalised).
Emission	(of a greenhouse gas). The release of greenhouse gases into the atmosphere. In all cases, this is the release of a waste by-product.
Emissions trading	See Chapter 3.
ENFO	The Environmental Information Service, 17 St. Andrew Street, Dublin 2. ENFO is a public information service on environmental matters, providing public access to wide-ranging and authoritative information on the environment. ENFO was established in September 1990 and is a service of the Department of the Environment and Local Government. Phone (01) 8882001 or lo-call 1890 200 191, fax (01) 8883946, website: http://www.enfo.ie/
Enteric fermentation	That part of the digestive process in ruminant animals (cows, sheep) where bacteria and other gut flora convert parts of the grass to a usable form for the animal; CH_4 is a by product and expelled from the animal.
EPA	Environmental Protection Agency. PO Box 3000, Johnstown Castle Estate, Co. Wexford. Phone (053) 60600, fax (053) 60699, website: http://www.epa.ie/
FIPS	Forest Inventory and Planning System.
Flexible mechanisms	See Kyoto mechanisms.
Fossil fuel	Peat, coal, fuels derived from crude oil (e.g. petrol and diesel) and natural gas are called fossil fuels because they have been formed over long periods of time from ancient organic matter. All contain varying amounts of carbon, and in the recovery of energy from the fuel through combustion in the presence of air, the carbon combines with the oxygen to form CO_2, which is vented to the atmosphere.
GDP	Gross Domestic Product.
Gothenburg Protocol (1999)	To the 1979 Convention on the Long-Range Transportation of Air Pollution to Abate Acidification, Eutrophication and Ground-Level Ozone. The Gothenburg Protocol requires reductions in emissions by 2010 in SO_2, NOx, Volatile Organic Compounds and Ammonia. See website: http://www.unece.org/env/lrtap/
Greenhouse gas	A gas in the atmosphere that freely allows radiation from the sun through to the earth's surface, but traps the heat radiated back from the earth's surface towards space and re-radiates it back to the earth's surface. The heating effect is analogous to the manner in which the glass of a greenhouse traps the sun's radiation to warm the air inside the greenhouse. Most greenhouse gases occur naturally and are a necessary part of the global climate system, but their concentrations can be increased by human action, causing climate change.
GWP	Greenhouse gases have different efficiencies in retaining solar energy in the atmosphere and also have different lifetimes in the atmosphere, before natural processes remove them. To compare the different greenhouse gases, emissions are calculated on the basis of their Global Warming Potential (GWP) over a normalised time horizon, giving a measure of their relative heating effect in the atmosphere. The 100 year time horizon (GWP100) is the one generally used and that provided for in relation to the Kyoto Protocol. The IPCC (1995) has developed these GWPs; all are expressed as GWP100:- CO_2 is the basic unit. (GWP of 1). CH_4 has a global warming potential equivalent to 21 units of CO_2, i.e. a GWP of 21. N_2O has a GWP of 310. Compounds in the HFC family have GWPs in the range 140 to 11,700. PFCs have GWPs in the range 6,500 to 9,200. SF_6 has a GWP of 23,900.
HCFCs	Hydrochlorofluorocarbons. A family of ozone depleting substances whose use is controlled under the Montreal Protocol on Substances that Deplete the Ozone Layer (1987, as amended). While HCFCs are also greenhouse gases, they are excluded from the UNFCCC and Kyoto Protocol as their use is controlled under the Montreal Protocol.
HFCs	Hydrofluorocarbons. See Industrial gases.
HGV	Heavy Goods Vehicle.
IEC	Irish Energy Centre, the national agency for energy efficiency and renewable energy information, advice and support. The Centre's mission is to promote the development of a sustainable national energy economy. Established in 1994 as an EU funded initiative of the Department of Public Enterprise. Address: Glasnevin, Dublin 9, Phone (01) 8369080, Energy Hotline 1850 376 666 (local call price), Fax: (01) 8372848, website, http://www.irish-energy.ie/
Industrial gases	The three non-natural greenhouse gases and gas families. HFCs (Hydrofluorocarbons), PFCs (Perfluorocarbons) and SF_6 (Sulphur Hexafluoride). These are more potent than the naturally occurring greenhouse gases and did not exist in the atmosphere before the industrial age. There are a number of individual HFCs and PFCs within these "families" of gases.
IPC	Integrated Pollution Control, in the context of licensing under the Environmental Protection Agency Act, 1992. To become IPPC licensing in line with EU Directive 96/61/EC.
IPCC	Intergovernmental Panel on Climate Change. This is the authoritative scientific source on human interference with the global climate system. Website at http://www.ipcc.ch/

IPPC	EU Integrated Pollution Prevention and Control Directive (96/61/EC).	**Party**	A country that has signed or ratified the UN Framework Convention on Climate Change or Kyoto Protocol, as appropriate. The EU is also a Party.
ISO 14001	International Standards Organisation quality standard for environmental management systems (1996).	**PFCs**	Perfluorocarbons. See Industrial gases.
JI	Joint Implementation (see end of Chapter 2).	**ppm**	Parts per million.
kt	Kilotonne (1,000 tonnes). 1,000 kt = 1 Mt	**Probiotics**	A live microbial feed supplement which beneficially affects the host animal by improving its intestinal microbial balance.
Kyoto mechanisms	The three flexibility measures that are provided for in the Kyoto Protocol viz Emissions Trading, JI (Joint Implementation) and the CDM (Clean Development Mechanism). See end Chapter 2 for JI and the CDM; Chapter 3 for Emissions Trading.	**PSO**	Public Service Obligation. An obligation placed on utility undertakings (generally in the energy sector) which takes account of general social, economic and environmental factors.
Kyoto Protocol	The second international agreement (1997) on climate change, setting binding limitation and reduction targets for developed countries. It is a protocol to the UN Framework Convention on Climate Change. Website of the Secretariat: http://www.unfccc.int/ Text of Protocol at http://www.unfccc.int/resource/convkp.html	**REPS**	Rural Environment Protection Scheme.
		Sequestration (of carbon)	The removal of CO_2 from the atmosphere and the storage of the carbon, generally by growing plants (e.g. by the fixing of carbon in the organic compounds which make up the body of a tree). It can include storage of carbon in associated soils and litter. Non-organic mechanisms for carbon sequestration are not considered by the Strategy.
LEAs	Local Energy Agencies	**Sink**	The reservoir in which sequestered CO_2 is stored, e.g. forestry. There are a number of natural sinks for CO_2 (e.g. the oceans, the natural biosphere) but sequestration by natural mechanisms is not relevant to the Kyoto Protocol.
Modal Shift	In the transport sector, move from the use of one *mode* of transport to another (e.g. greater use of public transport, rather than private cars for commuting).		
Montreal Protocol	*On Substances that Deplete the Ozone Layer* (1987, as amended). Imposes bans and controls on emissions that damage stratospheric ozone. See CFCs and HCFCs.	**SF$_6$**	Sulphur Hexafluoride. See Industrial gases.
		SMEs	Small and Medium-sized Enterprises.
Mt	Million Tonnes.	**SO$_2$**	Sulphur Dioxide. Implicated in acidification and other air pollution effects. Not controlled by the Kyoto Protocol, but significant reductions below 1990 levels are to be achieved under the Gothenburg Protocol. SO_2 is a by-product of the burning of many fossil fuels and measures implemented to control greenhouse gases require integration with measures to reduce SO_2.
MW	Megawatt = 1,000 kilowatts.		
MW$_e$	Megawatts of electricity.		
NDP	*National Development Plan 2000 – 2006.*		
N$_2$O	Nitrous Oxide. The third most important greenhouse gas. Naturally occurring and also arises from human activity.	**Tax Strategy Group (TSG)**	Advisory Committee on budgetary matters chaired by the Department of Finance.
"No regret" measures	See footnote 6 on page 21.	**Telematics**	Transport telematics provides the necessary information, communications and integration to help operators and travellers make better and coordinated decisions.
NOx	Nitrogen Oxides, viz NO (Nitrogen Oxide) and NO$_2$ (Nitrogen Dioxide). These are not greenhouse gases and are to be distinguished from N$_2$O. NOx is implicated in acidification and other air pollution effects. Not controlled by the Kyoto Protocol, but significant reductions below 1990 levels are to be achieved under the Gothenburg Protocol. NOx is a by-product of fuel combustion and measures implemented to control greenhouse gases from combustion require integration with measures to reduce NOx.	**TPER**	Total Primary Energy Requirement. A measure of all energy consumed nationally. It includes energy consumed in transformation (e.g. electricity generation and oil refining) as well as distribution processes.
		UNFCCC	UN Framework Convention on Climate Change, the first international agreement (1992) on action to tackle human induced climate change. Website of the Secretariat: http://www.unfccc.int/ Text of Convention at http://www.unfccc.int/resource/convkp.html
NRA	National Roads Authority.		
OECD	Organisation for Economic Cooperation and Development.	**VRT**	Vehicle Registration Tax.

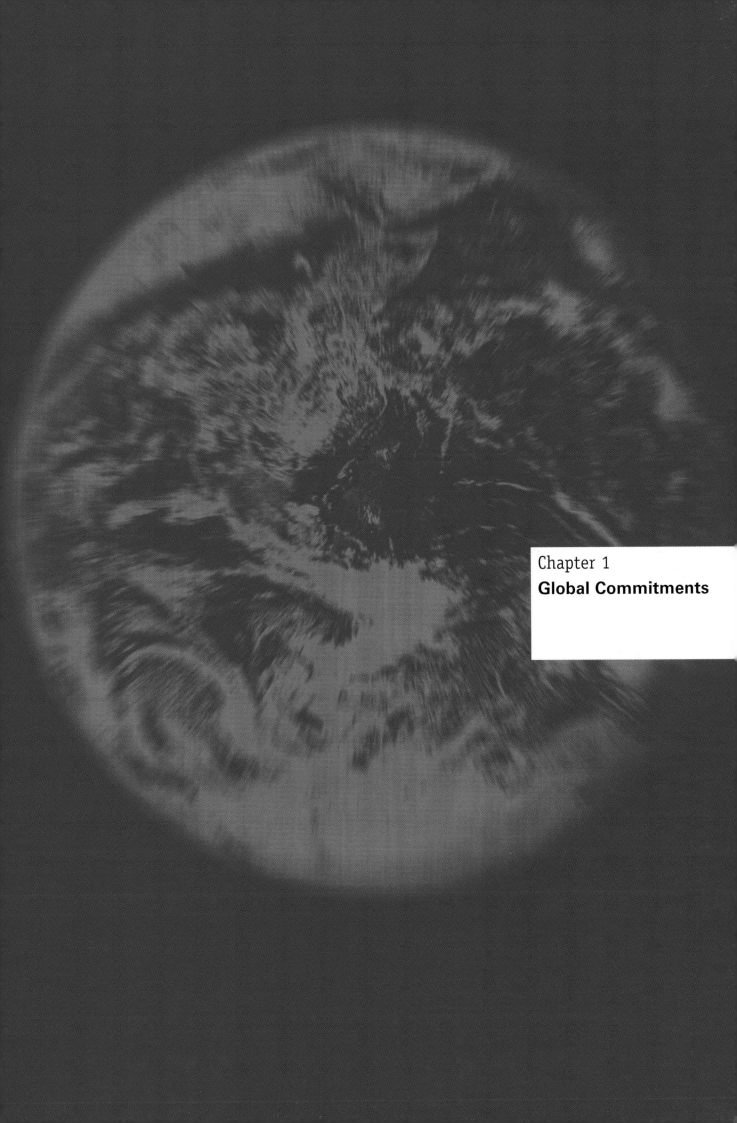

Chapter 1
Global Commitments

GLOBAL COMMITMENTS

Climate change is recognised as the most threatening global environmental problem facing humanity today. Ireland has a responsibility to future generations to limit greenhouse gas emissions as part of the overall international effort to tackle this threat.

The United Nations Framework Convention on Climate Change (UNFCCC), which Ireland signed at the "Earth Summit" in Rio de Janeiro in June 1992 and ratified in April 1994, is one of the most important environmental agreements with global application. It has been ratified by over 180 countries within a remarkably short space of time, and it is now, together with the Kyoto Protocol, a critical element in the framework for sustainable development policies at global, national and local levels.

In Kyoto in December 1997, developed countries agreed legally binding targets to achieve overall reductions of over 5% in net emissions of a basket of 6 greenhouse gases[1] in the period from 1990 to 2012. In Kyoto, the EU adopted the most ambitious reduction target, i.e. 8%, on the basis that targets for individual Member States would be differentiated to reflect differing economic and other circumstances (see EU "Bubble" on page 14). These targets represent the first step towards combating climate change and will pave the way for stronger commitments in the future.

IRELAND'S COMMITMENT

Irish emissions of greenhouse gases in 1990 were equivalent to 53.752 million tonnes (Mt) of carbon dioxide (CO_2). Due to the rapid economic growth which Ireland has enjoyed during the 1990s, and higher than expected population growth, current projections of CO_2 emissions for 2000 show an increase of 35.2% or 32.1% when counted on a net basis. Overall, Ireland's economic performance has resulted in higher emissions than expected and the necessary decoupling of growth in emissions from growth in the economy, becoming evident in the 1990s, has not been maintained.

In the period 2008 – 2012, Ireland's Kyoto commitment is to limit the net growth in emissions to 13% above 1990 levels, or to 60.74

Mt. CO_2 equivalent. Without the action set out in this Strategy, it is projected that net annual emissions would increase by up to 37.3% to 73.794 Mt CO_2 equivalent by 2010[2]. This essentially means that Ireland's target is to reduce emissions by up to 13.054 Mt CO_2 equivalent per annum for the commitment period 2008 – 2012.

Increased economic wealth places an onus on Ireland to take on – and ensures that we can afford – more ambitious climate change targets for the future. As a result, the key environmental challenge for Ireland over the next decade is to implement policies which will further decouple economic growth from growth in greenhouse gas emissions.

Kyoto Protocol Ratification

Ireland, with all other EU Member States, signed the Kyoto Protocol on 29 April 1998. The Protocol will enter into force when 55 Parties have ratified it, including developed country Parties accounting for at least 55% of the total 1990 CO_2 emissions from this industrialised group. Ireland will ratify the Protocol at the same time and on the same basis as the European Union and all Member States. In this regard, the EU supports ratification and entry into force of the Kyoto Protocol by 2002, the 10th anniversary of the Earth Summit in Rio de Janeiro, and other developed country Parties are also planning towards ratification to support this aim. This Strategy is an essential step in preparation for Ireland's ratification.

---

[1] The gases are carbon dioxide (CO_2), methane (CH_4), nitrous oxide (N_2O), hydrofluorocarbons (HFCs), perfluorocarbons (PFCs) and sulphur hexafluoride (SF_6). Emissions of these gases from human sources are covered by the Convention and Protocol; in the case of the Protocol, emissions may be offset against human-induced sequestration (absorption from the atmosphere) of carbon in forestry programmes. More details on emissions from the each sector of the economy and sinks (i.e. sequestration) are provided in the relevant Chapters and in Appendix 2.

[2] Throughout this Strategy, the projections shown are those deriving from official activity data prepared by Government Departments, and converted into emissions projections by the EPA. Appendix 2 deals with inventories and projections in more detail. These projections are the basis for identifying the necessary action to meet the national target.

THE KYOTO PROTOCOL PROVISIONS

Kyoto Commitments

The Kyoto Protocol sets targets for developed country Parties to achieve a 5.2% reduction in emissions of an aggregate of six greenhouse gases by 2008 – 2012 (referred to as the *first commitment period*) compared with 1990. The basket consists of the following gases: -

Greenhouse Gases Included

▸ carbon dioxide (CO_2)
▸ methane (CH_4)
▸ nitrous oxide (N_2O)

For most Parties, including all EU Member States, 1990 is the base year for this part of the basket

▸ hydrofluorocarbons (HFCs)
▸ perfluorocarbons (PFCs)
▸ sulphur hexafluoride (SF_6)

Ireland will select 1995 to be the base year for these gases, in common with the approach of most Parties.

Country Targets

A series of "differentiated" targets are set for individual Parties.

▸ 8% reduction for EU Member States and the European Community as a whole, most Economies in Transition (former Eastern Europe) and Switzerland;
▸ 7% reduction for the US;
▸ 6% reduction for Canada, Japan and Hungary;
▸ 5% reduction for Croatia;
▸ stabilisation at 1990 levels for New Zealand, Russia and the Ukraine;
▸ 1% increase for Norway;
▸ 8% increase for Australia; and
▸ 10% increase for Iceland.

The Protocol requires that by 2005 Parties must have made "demonstrable progress" towards achieving their commitments.

Sinks

The Protocol requires that Parties count some forestry activities (net removals of carbon by afforestation, reforestation and deforestation since 1990) towards meeting their targets. Absorption by sinks is measured as a verified change in carbon stocks. Methodological aspects of accounting for these sinks remain to be clarified and defined. Additional categories of human induced emissions from or sequestration by agricultural soils and in the land use change and forestry categories is being identified in ongoing negotiations: - it will be mandatory for Parties to include these in their inventories in the second and subsequent commitment periods (i.e. post 2012), but Parties may choose to incorporate them towards meeting their commitment for the first commitment period (2008 – 2012). Further clarity in relation to sinks is expected at COP6.

Policies and Measures

The Protocol includes a range of policies and measures for Parties to implement and/or further elaborate in accordance with national circumstances in achieving their target and in order to promote sustainable development. These include:-

▸ enhanced energy efficiency;
▸ protection and enhancement of sinks;
▸ promotion of sustainable agriculture;
▸ R&D in the areas of renewable and new forms of energy, sequestration technologies and advanced environmentally sound technologies;
▸ removal of subsidies, taxes and exemptions that run counter to the application of market instruments;
▸ reform in all sectors, including transport, to limit or reduce greenhouse gas emissions;
▸ CH_4 reductions in the waste and energy sectors.

Provision is made also for international co-operation to enhance the effectiveness of action at the level of an individual country.

Use of Market Mechanisms ("Kyoto Mechanisms")

Parties may meet part of their targets through flexible mechanisms, viz., international emissions trading, joint implementation (JI), and the Clean Development Mechanism (CDM). Emissions trading can take place between Parties with quantified limitation or reduction targets (referred to as Annex I Parties); JI is project-based emissions trading which can occur through bilateral arrangements between Annex I Parties, and the CDM is project-based "trading" which can take place between Annex I Parties and developing country Parties.

The Kyoto Protocol provides that emissions trading and the other flexible mechanisms must be supplemental to domestic action. The rules, modalities and guidelines for the use of these flexible mechanisms are still under negotiation, with COP6 to provide further clarification.

EU "Bubble"

The Protocol provides that the European Community and the Member States may achieve the EU 8% reduction target jointly. A "burden sharing" agreement has been reached on the distribution of this overall target between all Member States, taking into account a number of factors such as projections for future greenhouse gas emissions, including economic growth factors, and relative efforts required to meet the Kyoto target, so as to achieve an equitable distribution of the overall burden involved. Under this arrangement, Ireland has agreed a national target to limit the increase in its greenhouse gas emissions to 13% above 1990 levels in the period 2008 – 2012. The national target reflects a number of factors, including the relatively underdeveloped state of the economy in the base year (1990), as well as subsequent economic growth, available projections for greenhouse gas emissions and anticipated wealth by the commitment period. The targets for each Member State reflect their particular national circumstances.

SCIENCE OF CLIMATE CHANGE

The **Intergovernmental Panel on Climate Change** (IPCC) was established in 1988 by the UN Environment Programme (UNEP) and the World Meteorological Organisation (WMO) at the UN General Assembly's instructions to examine the emerging science of climate change. The IPCC first reported in 1990, concluding that human-induced climate change is a *real* threat. In concluding *"the balance of evidence suggests a discernible human influence on global climate"*, the Second Assessment Report3 (1995) noted that global *"climate is expected to continue to change in the future"*. Further detail on the Second Assessment Report, and the global impacts of climate change, are in Appendix 1.

IMPACTS OF CLIMATE CHANGE ON IRELAND[4]

The predicted potential impacts of climate change on Ireland are both positive and negative. While many of the impacts would be disruptive and potentially very costly, none (apart from the loss of peatlands) are likely to be on a par with the worst impacts elsewhere in the world. Examples of the projected impacts in Ireland, based on scenarios generally within the range predicted in the IPCC Second Assessment Report, include: -

▶ Significant increases in winter rainfall, with the average winter water levels in rivers, lakes and soils higher than at present, and with serious flooding more frequent. Areas now subject to flooding would suffer flooding of greater severity and duration; areas currently flood-free would suffer occasional floods.

▶ Lower summer rainfall causing regular water shortages, especially in the midlands, east and north, and affecting both people and ecosystems. There would be less recharge of reservoirs during the summer; water shortages would occur regularly and would be longer than at present. The change in rainfall patterns could cause regular water deficits in peatlands, leading to accelerated erosion and loss of sphagnum-based bogs. Loss of bogland is likely to be the single most significant impact on Ireland and would be without remedy.

▶ Rising sea levels and more storm events and storm surges, particularly on the West Coast, with storms of a greater severity; approximately 176,000ha (2.5% of the land area of the State) are at risk from rising sea levels, including related erosion, flooding and environmental change. The most significant problem in this regard is the impact of storms, where even under conditions of slight sea-level rise, the statistical recurrence of extreme events associated with storms falls dramatically. Within a lifetime, an extreme weather event, which in 1990 might be expected to occur every 100 years, might be expected to occur every 5 years. Most of the area likely to be affected is on the West Coast, but the most vulnerable areas are likely to be on the East Coast.

▶ Areas of the coast subject to human development would be most at risk, and could suffer loss of infrastructure. Human use of the coast is quite intensive, and low lying areas of all coastal cities are highly developed with several key industries (energy, chemicals), sea-related activities (ports), and residential development under potential threat. Protective options include abandonment of land, stronger planning

---

[3] Summary for Policymakers available at http://www.ipcc.ch/pub/reports.htm
[4] The scenarios analysed in *Climate Change: Studies on the Implications for Ireland* (Brendan McWilliams editor, published in 1991 by the Department of the Environment) were based on *Climate Change - The IPCC Scientific Assessment* (1990), also known as the IPCC First Assessment Report.

controls, and fiscal disincentives for coastal development. While the costs of sea level rise are largely unquantifiable in the absence of information on replacement costs, the alternative of building all necessary hard engineered or protective sea defences to protect all vulnerable coast would cost in the order of £270bn (1990 prices). Other alternatives, including abandonment of land, fiscal or financial penalties for coastal development, or softer non-engineering protective measures would have to be considered.

- Increased agricultural production, with new crops becoming viable and agricultural production costs reduced if prolonged summer droughts do not become a problem. Grass growth could enjoy beneficial effects with an increase of 20% possible with higher temperatures and changes in rainfall patterns. New grassland and livestock management systems would be possible, with a longer grazing season and the prospect of growing additional forage crops (e.g. maize, fodder beet, lucerne). There would be little or no increase in cereal yields, but increases in other crops are possible, and the area for growth of many arable crops would migrate northwards. A number of new crops (e.g. sunflower) may become viable in the South and Southeast.

- Some existing forestry species may suffer (e.g. where availability of water and nitrogen are limiting factors), with others becoming more productive (higher temperatures and increased CO_2 concentrations in the atmosphere supporting higher rates of photosynthesis and hence higher growth rates).

- Both agriculture and forestry would be threatened by additional pests and diseases. However, they would have time to plan strategic responses as more information becomes available.

See also Appendix 1, for global impacts of climate change.

A new assessment of the impact of climate change on Ireland will be undertaken and the EPA is considering research proposals in this regard. The assessment will, inter alia, be based on the findings of the Third Assessment Report by the IPCC, due to be published in 2001. It will include assessment of the full costs of failure to take action, the costs of non-compliance with the Kyoto Protocol and the costs of adaptation to climate change.

It is recognised that Ireland cannot, on its own, prevent or ameliorate the impacts of climate change. It is, however, necessary to meet, in partnership with our partners in the EU and the global community, our responsibilities to prevent dangerous human interference with the global climate system.

SOURCES OF GREENHOUSE GAS EMISSIONS

All economic activity that requires energy consumption, as well as certain non-energy activities in areas such as agriculture, produces greenhouse gases. The principle sources in Ireland are: -

Contribution to National Emissions (2010 Projections assuming no action)

Energy: - The energy sector is the largest source of Ireland's CO_2 emissions, from fossil fuel combustion in the production of electricity. Small emissions of CH_4 also occur from pipeline leakage in the transmission of gas and some N_2O is formed in fuel combustion.

1990: 21.6% of all greenhouse gases
1998: 24.6%
2010: 25.0%
(Emissions from consumption of electricity excluded from emissions in other sectors below)

Transport: - The primary emission in this sector is CO_2 as a result of fuel combustion, and some N_2O is produced in combustion and catalytic converters. Transport is generally proving to be the most difficult sector in which to achieve controls on greenhouse gas emissions in most countries, due to rising vehicle numbers and increasing travel.

1990: 9.5% of all greenhouse gases
1998: rising to 14.3%
2010: rising further to 18.9%

Industry: - The industrial sector mainly contributes to greenhouse gas emissions through energy use, including direct consumption of fossil fuels and use of electricity, and through emissions from a number of industrial processes (e.g. CO_2 is a by-product of cement manufacture, N_2O in the fertiliser industry). This sector is also the source of emissions of the industrial gases HFCs and PFCs (electronics and medical sectors).

1990: 13.5% of all greenhouse gases
1998: 13.6%
2010: 14.6%

Agriculture: - Agricultural emissions of greenhouse gases are very significant in the Irish context. Agriculture is the largest source of CH_4 and N_2O, with the main sources being enteric fermentation (ruminant digestion) in the livestock herd (CH_4) andagricultural soils and manures (N_2O). Cattle are the dominant source of CH_4. The quantity of nitrogenous fertiliser spread and the breakdown of this in the soil is the main determinant of the amount of N_2O emitted from agriculture.

1990: 34.6% of all greenhouse gases
1998: falling somewhat to 32.0%
2010: projected to fall further to 25.6%

Built Environment, Commercial/Institutional and Residential Sectors: - Emissions of greenhouse gases attributable to these sectors are almost exclusively CO_2, from energy use consumed domestically for space heating, etc. and electricity consumed in appliances. Small amounts of CH_4 and N_2O associated with fuel consumption are also emitted.

1990: 17.6% of all greenhouse gases
1998: 15%
2010: 14.4%

Local Authorities and Waste: - Emissions from waste are primarily of CH_4, which arise from the anaerobic decomposition, in landfill, of wastes containing carbon.

1990: 3.3% of all greenhouse gases
1998: 2.5%
2010: 1.5%

Forestry: - While most economic activity can contribute to emissions, the Forestry Sector can sequester carbon by removing CO_2 from the atmosphere as part of the natural forest growth cycle. A change in land use from livestock-based agriculture to forestry can ensure a double benefit of additional CO_2 sequestration with an accompanied reduction in CH_4 and N_2O emissions.

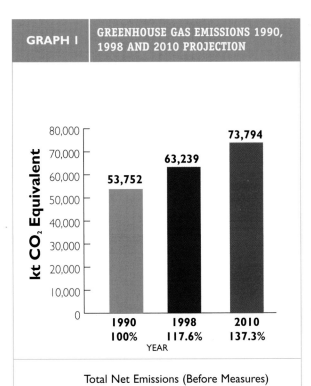

GRAPH I	GREENHOUSE GAS EMISSIONS 1990, 1998 AND 2010 PROJECTION

Total Net Emissions (Before Measures)

STRATEGIC FRAMEWORK

This Strategy provides a framework for firm and continuing climate change abatement action. It also provides the framework for achieving the necessary reductions in emissions in the most efficient and equitable manner while continuing both to support economic growth, and prepare Ireland for the more ambitious reductions after 2012. Meeting the challenge will provide a major opportunity to incorporate sustainable development considerations into how we do business, while maintaining an efficient and productive economy. New technologies and options will be encouraged to evolve, to exploit the business opportunities involved, reinforce quality of life, and contribute importantly towards sustainable development across the economy and society.

Comprehensive economic and environmental analysis for purposes of this Strategy, undertaken in 1998[5], took account of the range of available analytical work at national and international levels. The Strategy also takes account of further economic analysis at a sectoral level, including in particular, for purposes of the *Green Paper on Sustainable Energy*[6] (1999) .

The Strategy is a radical departure from "business as usual": - As the challenge of addressing climate change requires radical change in the manner of doing business, underlying priorities for future development will also require significant alterations. Achieving this quantum shift will be challenging, and will require a concerted effort over a significant period.

A premium is placed on the pursuit of sustainable development: - In particular, sustainable energy development requires maximum efficiency in the industrial, commercial and domestic sectors and intensified decoupling of energy and transport growth from economic growth. Agricultural emissions will be managed by a combination of measures including controls on animal numbers, reduced fertiliser use and increased support for forestry.

The Strategy will accommodate unique and dynamic features of the economy: - For example, Ireland does not have a heavy industrial base, but has a higher intensity of fossil fuel emissions compared to countries with more scope for large-scale hydro power or which use nuclear energy. Ireland also has the highest proportion of greenhouse gas emissions from agriculture in the EU.

17

[5] *"Limitation and Reduction of CO_2 and other Greenhouse Gas Emissions in Ireland"*, (ERM in association with ESRI & Byrne Ó Cléirigh (June 1998) commissioned by the Departments of the Environment and Local Government, and Public Enterprise). Available on the internet at http://www.environ.ie/environ/env5.html
[6] Available at http://www.irlgov.ie/tec/energy/renewinfo.htm

Action will be taken in all sectors: - This will require citizens, consumers, business and economic sectors to make daily environmentally sustainable choices to ensure that Ireland's commitment is successfully achieved.

Action will be taken early: - Early action, having regard to environment and cost effectiveness considerations, is a cornerstone of the policies and measures in this Strategy. Delay would require more painful action at a later date to address both Kyoto compliance and stronger future commitments. Where Ireland can achieve reductions beyond those required for the first commitment period (2008 – 2012) these will be banked for use in the second and subsequent commitment periods to assist in meeting the more rigorous targets expected in the post-2012 period.

Action will be developed on a cost effective basis: - To maximise economic efficiency and protect competitiveness within a sustainable development framework, emphasis will be placed, in the context of specific sectoral measures, on identifying and implementing least cost options to achieve reductions and on identification of opportunities for compensatory action.

Use will be made of the international economic instruments in the Kyoto Protocol, including international emissions trading: - These mechanisms offer opportunities to identify and participate in least cost reductions, reducing the overall economic cost of achieving our Kyoto commitment.

Chapter 2
**National Climate
Change Strategy**

OBJECTIVES

The objectives of this Strategy are to: -

▶ meet Ireland's legally binding commitment under the Kyoto Protocol in accordance with Articles 3 and 4 of the Protocol, and accordingly to limit the net increase in Ireland's greenhouse gas emissions to 13% above 1990 levels[7] in the period 2008 – 2012,

▶ position Ireland to meet potentially more ambitious targets in the post-2012 period.

The Government recognises that: -

▶ a broad range of policies and measures, including measures tailored specifically to reducing emissions from individual sectors,

▶ economic instruments with broad sectoral and/or cross-sectoral application,

▶ common and coordinated policies and measures implemented at EU and wider international levels, and

▶ participation to the extent possible in the Kyoto mechanisms,

are necessary contributions to the achievement of Ireland's commitments under the Kyoto Protocol.

AMBITION OF THE OBJECTIVES

The Government is satisfied that: -

▶ Ireland's greenhouse gas emissions growth limitation target is **environmentally necessary** as an initial contribution to the global task of tackling climate change, given the need for early action towards the longer-term global measures necessary to avoid the detrimental effects of climate change; these are expected to occur at accelerating rates if no, or inadequate, steps are taken.

▶ The Strategy ensures **balanced action** over time; many of its policies and measures have long lead-times before the structural changes involved can reduce greenhouse gas emissions. Progressive action must be taken if Ireland is to (a) have made demonstrable progress towards our target by 2005, (b) meet the target itself in the period 2008 – 2012, and (c) provide a sound basis for continuing and more intensive action post-2012.

▶ Ireland's target is **environmentally ambitious** in the context of rapid economic growth and the action necessary to ensure that this growth is environmentally sustainable. Strong emphasis is placed on accelerated decoupling of the link between economic growth and greenhouse gas emissions that is already evident in Ireland and other advanced economies.

▶ This Strategy is **technically achievable.** It is clear from the full list of available policies and measures at domestic level, the ability of the EU to develop common and coordinated policies and measures, and access to the flexible mechanisms of the Kyoto Protocol, that the national target can be achieved. It is the aim of the Strategy to do so in a manner that promotes sustainable development, achieves sectoral equity and supports economic development having regard to competitiveness considerations.

▶ Early action can focus on the **adoption of existing technologies** and the implementation of policies and measures shown to be successful in more mature economies. Over the longer-term, climate change abatement can underpin, not dislocate, economic growth by acting as a catalyst for the development and adoption of new technologies, and encouraging technological innovation to address the more substantial emissions reductions that will be necessary into the future.

▶ The Strategy is **economically achievable**, both overall and by sector, as it distributes the effort required in regard to all sources of greenhouse gas emissions (and sequestration of carbon from the atmosphere) across all sectors of the economy, maximising the options for low and no-cost reductions, generating additional efficiencies in the economy and positioning Irish industry to take advantage of the increasing scope for growth in a global economy that will both demand, and increasingly rely on, sustainable development.

▶ The policies and measures incorporated in this Strategy are consistent with **international best practice**. Many countries already have the range of measures set out in this Strategy (regulatory, awareness raising, incentives, economic instruments etc., adapted to meet national requirements) in place or in the course of preparation.

[7] 1995 base year for HFCs, PFCs and SF_6

GUIDING PRINCIPLES

Promotion of Sustainable Development

Tackling climate change is a critical test for sustainable development policies. The ultimate objective of the UNFCCC is to ensure the "*stabilisation of greenhouse gas concentrations in the atmosphere at a level that would prevent dangerous anthropogenic interference with the climate system*". The concept of sustainability requires development to be within the capacity of the environment to support it without suffering lasting damage or depletion. It places strong emphasis, therefore, on the pressures arising from intensive exploitation and depletion of natural resources, transformation and transportation of increasing quantities of energy and materials, and growing production and consumption. At its broadest, sustainable development requires co-operation in the use of world resources in a way that benefits the global environment and the economies of developing countries.

National sustainable development policy is grounded on: -

▸ the **precautionary principle**, which requires that appropriate action be taken where significant evidence of environmental risk exists, and places emphasis on dealing with the causes, rather than the results, of environmental damage;

▸ the **integration** of environmental considerations into other policies as a fundamental means of decoupling economic growth and environmental degradation and promoting economic and environmental efficiency;

▸ the **polluter pays principle**, which correctly allocates the costs of pollution, energy consumption and environmental resource use, and the production and disposal of waste to the responsible polluters and consumers, rather than to society at large or future generations. Cost internalisation, including through market-based economic and fiscal instruments, provides a more balanced and full measurement of national growth and prosperity;

▸ **shared responsibility**, which requires broadly based involvement by public bodies, private enterprise and the general public to achieve sustainable development objectives;

▸ **social equity**, which requires that sustainable development must be achieved in the context of policies which reduce poverty and social exclusion and build an inclusive society.

It is against the yardstick of the ultimate objective of the UNFCCC that climate change commitments are assessed. A safe concentration level of greenhouse gases in the atmosphere should be achieved in a timeframe which allows ecosystems to adapt naturally to climate change, ensures that food production is not threatened and enables economic development to proceed in a sustainable manner.

Sectoral Equity

The burden borne across the economy must be equitable. The Strategy is designed to ensure that the economic burden arising for any sector will not be disproportionate, and the monitoring and review mechanisms put in place will assess the relative impacts on sectors of the economy and society to ensure equity. Criteria and considerations towards the achievement of sectoral equity will also include: -

▸ the relative effort in each sector to achieve reductions below business as usual, based on an examination of the full economic cost of the relevant policies and measures, both at a sectoral level and across the economy;

▸ a preference for implementing "no regret" policies and measures[8] in the first instance;

▸ the adoption of all economically feasible options for reductions in a sector;

▸ the use of cross-sectoral economic instruments such as a combination of emissions trading and greenhouse gas taxation, as incentives to identify least-cost options within and between sectors;

▸ achievement of a balance between the operation of cross-sectoral measures such as emissions trading and taxation on the one hand, and sector-specific measures on the other, to avoid disproportionate costs for any economic actor in the economy;

▸ the implementation of alternative – potentially higher cost – policies and measures by sectors which do not utilise available "least cost" options;

▸ the allocation of national emissions to sectors engaged in emissions trading will be sufficiently below business as usual projections having regard to the circumstances of each sector so that the sectors make an effective and equitable contribution to meeting the national target.

Where the non-implementation of "no regret" and "least cost" policies and measures in the first instance can be attributed to market failure, any education, information or communications barriers which may hinder the uptake or effectiveness of low-cost options will be addressed. Where appropriate, regard will also be had to the cost of compensatory measures in the other sectors where economically advantageous measures are not undertaken

---

[8] In this Strategy, "no regrets" policies and measures include:-
▸ those that achieve immediate savings;
▸ those where savings can be made on the basis of returns on investment at or better that commercial rates; and
▸ those where adaptation to maximise emissions reductions and limitations is made to policies and measures necessary for other reasons.
In certain cases, the savings will not be achieved at the firm or sector making the investment, and in certain cases, support from State agencies (e.g. advice on the identification of potential for savings, awareness raising) will be necessary.

in a given sector due to other policy considerations.

Protection of Economic Development and Competitiveness

The Irish economy has enjoyed very rapid rates of economic growth over recent years, and continued economic growth of the order of 5% per annum over the period of the *National Development Plan 2000 – 2006* (NDP) is predicted. Ireland's competitive position is influenced by a range of factors including wage rates, a highly educated young workforce and a commitment to the encouragement of investment in growth sectors in the global economy. A high quality environment is also a key factor in promoting knowledge-based high value-added projects, with their demand for qualified employees.

Economic growth has **not** been dependent on low costs in sectors with high greenhouse gas emissions, such as the energy and agriculture sectors[9]. It is recognised that increases in the price of any factor of production affecting Ireland more than other countries will have some effect on competitiveness. However, where costs increase, our relative competitive position will receive a level of protection through the need for trading partners to take actions within their economies to meet their Kyoto commitments. In the implementation of the Strategy, regard will be had to the recommendations of the National Competitiveness Council in regard to achieving sustained improvement in international competitiveness rankings.

Competitiveness is a moving target in a changing context[10]. The successful adaptation to continuing change is the dynamic expression of competitiveness: - it is clear that once the Kyoto Protocol enters into force and implementation of the necessary measures to meet national targets gathers pace, one of the main drivers of international environmental and economic policy will be climate change. The Government is satisfied that the initiation of early action in Ireland will assist in preparing the economy to meet these competitiveness challenges.

Ireland will also vigorously support the adoption of common and coordinated policies and measures, within the EU and under the Protocol, including supporting relevant harmonisation of tax and other measures to implement the EU abatement strategy.

Further protection of competitiveness will be achieved by taking those steps which are least-cost, and using market-based instruments to assist affected sectors identify and benefit from the cheapest mitigation options. Economic instruments, which generate cost and other efficiencies, also create an incentive to better environmental performance, and can assist in promoting technological innovation and developing and exploiting new markets and potential opportunities. Particular emphasis was placed in the Technology Foresight programme on energy technologies that support new and renewable sources of energy, energy efficiency and optimisation of energy consumption.

Maximising Economic Efficiency

Policies and measures across all sectors, together with "no-regret" measures, are necessary to maximise the economic and social efficiency of the Strategy. A range of "no-regret" measures, i.e. policies that reduce greenhouse gas emissions or sequester carbon at no or low economic cost, and in some cases which have positive economic benefits has been identified. Some of these measures may have costs for individual sectors, but weakening such measures is likely to add to overall costs, as the emissions reductions not achieved through "no-regret" measures will have to be paid for at a higher cost elsewhere in the economy. It is also essential that "no-regret" options be utilised wherever possible to reduce the burden to sectors of the economy which are expected to implement policies and measures with some cost.

Use of cross-sectoral economic instruments and market mechanisms will enable sectors to identify the most cost-efficient options and mechanisms, and allow those with significant costs to identify and implement the lowest cost options available to them.

In using economic instruments, priority will be given to measures designed to remove existing distortionary direct and indirect taxes, tax provisions and subsidies (explicit and implicit) that have negative or perverse environmental impacts. Accordingly, economically efficient policy options will have additional environmental benefits, which will be taken into account so that the true impact of implementing the Strategy can be identified.

Meeting Long-Term and Future Commitments

Ireland must take determined action now to curb the growth of greenhouse gas emissions. In addition to the priority attaching to our environmental responsibilities in this area, legal obligations initiated by the Kyoto Protocol are likely to intensify in future years. Intensification of existing action, and additional action beyond that contained in this Strategy, will be required as a result.

▶ The first review of commitments under the Protocol is

---

[9] The National Competitiveness Council in their *Annual Competitiveness Reports* (1998 and 1999), and NESC in *Opportunities, Challenges and Capacities for Choice* (December 1999) identified the key economic factors which have enhanced Ireland's competitive position in recent years, and confirms they are the key to Ireland's economic and competitive success. These include labour costs and productivity; education levels, policy and performance; training; technological innovation and performance; trade; investment and financial markets; environmental status and monitoring; and infrastructure, particularly transport and telecommunications.
[10] NESC in *Opportunities, Challenges and Capacities for Choice* (December 1999).

expected about 2 years after its entry into force to lead to negotiation of additional commitments. The Kyoto Protocol also provides that negotiations on commitments for the post-2012 period must begin at least 7 years earlier, i.e. by 2005.

▶ Without substantive action now, the costs of adapting to the impacts of climate change, including in parts of the developing world where these can least be met, will rise significantly.

▶ Substantive action is needed now to ensure also that future generations are not burdened with either additional costs to reduce emissions or the costs of having to adapt to the dangerous impacts of climate change, costs which would be reduced through early action now.

▶ Current and anticipated economic growth, at consistently higher levels than in other industrialised countries, will mean that Ireland will be one of the wealthiest economies by 2013. Furthermore, with a growth limitation – rather than a stabilisation or reduction – target in the period to 2012, and with most other EU and OECD countries with a reduction target in the same timeframe, Ireland will be close to the upper end of global emissions intensity in 2013. In this context, it must also be recognised that the Irish economy currently is one of the highest fossil fuel intensive economies in the world, with low penetration of renewables such as large-scale hydro and no access to nuclear energy. Additionally, with a significantly higher proportion of our overall basket of gases deriving from agriculture, Irish emissions, even when the Kyoto target is attained, will be comparatively very high in EU terms and comparable with average emissions levels from the most greenhouse gas intensive OECD economies.

Alongside the immediate importance of achieving our Kyoto target, successful implementation of the measures identified in this Strategy, complemented by actions at EU level through common and coordinated measures, will position Ireland well for a more rigorous regime thereafter.

Impetus to Early Action

Early action is essential. Not undertaking action as soon as practicable and on a progressive basis could involve meeting large reductions very abruptly in the commitment period, adding to the potential costs of achieving the required reductions. There are potential disincentives to early action: -

▶ legally binding commitments do not arise until 2008 – 2012;

▶ policy conflicts at a sectoral and inter-sectoral level;

▶ uncertainty as to when competitor firms will take action;

▶ a desire to delay early actions with cheap reduction potential for a number of reasons, for example, to save low cost

reductions for a later stage to reduce the costs of complying with tax requirements when implemented, or to maximise emissions allocations under an emissions trading system.

The appropriate balance and timing of measures must be achieved. The *Green Paper on Sustainable Energy* sets out a number of considerations to be taken into account in the energy sector. These will be evaluated in determining the optimal timing for action, and similar considerations will arise in relation to other sectors. In this evaluation process, the cost to the economy of **not** taking early action will be factored in.

Policies and measures, in particular cross-sectoral economic instruments such as emissions trading, will be implemented in a manner that recognises the initiative of sectors/companies taking early action in support of this Strategy. In a number of instances, past action has already contributed to the limitation of greenhouse gas emissions, for example through the implementation of energy efficiency measures in industry, even though greenhouse gas emissions reductions has not been the driving force behind the actions.

INTERNATIONAL CONSIDERATIONS

Support for Common and Coordinated Policies and Measures

While the UNFCCC and the Kyoto Protocol define the overall context for action, important elements of the policy framework are also set at EU level. In addition to the burden sharing agreement to meet the overall EU 8% reduction target through comparable effort across Member States, priority action at European level on common and coordinated policies and measures will assist the achievement of national targets within a balanced competitive climate. These common and coordinated policies and measures at EU level are important to achieve the national commitment.

The European Council of Environment Ministers has invited the Commission to take forward proposals for common measures in a wide range of areas across all sectors including fuel subsidies and taxation, energy market liberalisation and CAP reform. Climate change policy has also been highlighted as a priority in the context of work at EU level to advance environmental integration. However, given the lack of certainty regarding the scale and timing of reductions through action at a common and coordinated level within the EU, due to the dependence on agreement on the scale and timing of such action, it is necessary to focus chiefly on domestic action in the Strategy.

The European Commission is actively developing common and coordinated policies and measures within the EU, and in the European Climate Change Programme. The Government will continue strongly to support the development and implementation of appropriate common and coordinated policies and measures to assist Member States achieve their targets and to ensure the integration of climate concerns in all policy areas. Ongoing development of taxation measures in other EU countries, and their intensification to meet Kyoto targets, will afford Ireland an opportunity to accelerate and intensify taxation as a cross-sectoral measure in a manner compatible with the maintenance of competitiveness.

Participation in International Mechanisms

The Kyoto Protocol provides for three flexible mechanisms: -

▸ International Emissions Trading (IET) (dealt with in more detail in Chapter 3),

▸ Joint Implementation (JI) – a project-based instrument which allows Parties with defined targets to share reduction credits where one Party invests in a project in the territory of another with the aim of reducing emissions or enhancing sinks.

▸ Clean Development Mechanism (CDM) – a project-based instrument similar to JI which allows developed country Parties gain reduction credits for investments in appropriate projects in the developing world. In the CDM, the project must satisfy a number of additional criteria that specifically benefit sustainable development in the host Party, and a share of the proceeds arising from project activities must go towards assisting developing countries that are particularly vulnerable to the adverse effects of climate change to meet cost of adaptation.

The negotiations to agree the detailed principles, rules, modalities and guidelines for the operation of these mechanisms should be finalised in November 2000 at COP6 of the Convention. Entity level participation in these mechanisms is likely to be agreed, and the Government will support this approach within the overall EU negotiating position.

The Government recognises the value of firms making investments under JI and the CDM. In an open and transparent international market, Irish firms can expect to have equal access to investment opportunities, especially in the case of firms already making investment choices overseas. Where firms acquire emission reduction units (JI) or certified emissions reductions (CDM), they will be able to offset these against their objectives under the Strategy subject to the internationally agreed rules for the operation of these mechanisms. Where firms acquire certified emissions reductions under the CDM in respect of the period 2000 – 2008, these will not be incorporated into any calculation of their obligation towards the national commitment (i.e. there will be no penalty for early action under the CDM).

An examination of development assistance made by Ireland in the Third World will also be undertaken by the Department of Foreign Affairs to identify how much, if any, of this is appropriate to be included in the CDM, or can be adjusted to become part of the CDM. The priority for this assistance **will not** be adjusted for purely domestic climate change and emissions reductions reasons, but where synergies exist between meeting the national target and the priorities of the countries where investment is undertaken, these will be pursued to the mutual benefit of Ireland and that country.

Joint Implementation in Ireland

It is likely that this mechanism will be used mostly in respect of investment by OECD countries in countries in transition to a market economy (i.e. Eastern Europe and the countries that were part of the former Soviet Union). Irish firms may be amongst those benefiting from this mechanism through suitable investment. However, as Ireland attracts significant inward investment, provision for JI sharing of reductions in emissions achieved may be put forward as part of future investment proposals. The Government will operate on the presumption that such proposals, by limiting the level of reductions achieved by such projects that may be counted towards achieving the national target, will add to the overall economic cost of compliance with our Kyoto obligations. Accordingly, the Government will require, inter alia, that an assessment of the implications for the cost of compliance with the Kyoto obligation will be undertaken before any JI project is based in Ireland.

Chapter 3
**Cross-Sectoral
Instruments**

CROSS-SECTORAL INSTRUMENTS

Cross-sectoral market-based instruments will be used to provide an across-the-board incentive for a wide range of actions to reduce emissions. The Kyoto target cannot be met by actions in one, or indeed in a limited number of sectors; equity requires that equivalent action be taken across all sectors.

Article 2 of the Kyoto Protocol requires that Parties

"Implement and/or further elaborate policies and measures in accordance with national circumstances, such as:...progressive reduction or phasing out of market imperfections, fiscal incentives, tax and duty exemptions that run counter to the objective of the Convention and application of market instruments"

Economic instruments comprise a variety of measures which use market processes to achieve objectives. These include measures to change prices of goods or services, and the development of markets (in carbon or greenhouse gas emissions) where they do not currently exist. Distinctive features of economic instruments, increasing their utility in a climate change abatement context, include: -

▸ mobilisation of market forces towards the achievement of the Kyoto target and reduced need for direct Government intervention in different sectors of the economy;

▸ working through price mechanisms to attach a price to greenhouse gas emissions which will need to be recovered in the final price of product;

▸ creating incentives for firms to reduce emissions in the most efficient and cost-effective manner;

▸ enabling decision makers to choose between reducing their environmental impacts or facing higher production costs;

▸ providing, through efficient markets, continuing dynamic incentives to reduce emissions and maximise the competitive advantages of achieving low cost reductions in emissions;

▸ encouraging and rewarding innovative behaviour through environmentally responsible cost avoidance and profit making;

▸ ability to promote continuous, rather than once-off, improvements in greenhouse gas efficiencies.

The two main market-based cross-sectoral instruments are the **trading** of and the **taxation** of greenhouse gas emissions.

EMISSIONS TRADING

Agreement on the necessary prerequisites for international emissions trading is expected to be reached at COP6 in November 2000. Ireland, within the overall EU negotiating position, is supporting the development of an international emissions trading regime that is environmentally effective, economically efficient, transparent and open in operation, and capable of actually achieving the reductions promised by the process. This will require strong domestic and international monitoring and review and an effective compliance regime, including appropriate penalties for non-compliance.

International emissions trading provides a mechanism to enable Parties to ensure precise compliance with their commitments, and Ireland will participate actively in the Kyoto flexible mechanisms from their inception. It is expected that international emissions trading may be carried out at intergovernmental level (Governments will, in any event, remain legally responsible for achievement of their Kyoto commitments), but most Parties may empower individual firms and utilities to participate in the international market, making the private sector the main operators in the market.

Firms would have the ability to sell emissions on a domestic or international market (if they can cheaply over-achieve the reductions required of them) and others would have the ability to purchase emissions domestically and internationally, if they are unable to meet their legally binding limits established as part of the trading arrangements "in house" in a cost effective manner. An efficient and transparent market in emissions would determine, through the price mechanism, the cost of achieving Ireland's national target.

Emissions Trading Advisory Group

In 1998, the Minister for the Environment and Local Government established an expert advisory group on the potential of emissions trading with terms of reference to examine and advise him on the options involved and the Irish negotiating position on international trading. The report of the group is being published with the Strategy, with a view to informing potential participants on the options and choices involved in the development of international emissions trading.

European Commission Green Paper on Trading[11]

The European Commission has launched a discussion on emissions trading in the EU, and its Green Paper notes there is a good case for the development of a pilot trading scheme by 2005 to prepare for implementation of trading under the Kyoto Protocol in 2008. The Commission also recognises that, for a number of reasons relating e.g. to the internal market, State aids, competitiveness, reducing administrative and regulatory disparities between Member States, and ensuring overall compliance, a

---

[11] COM (00)87 of 8 March 2000 *"Green Paper on greenhouse gas emissions trading within the European Union"*
Available at http://europa.eu.int/comm/environment/docum/0087_en.htm

Community-wide approach to trading may be appropriate. Many questions relating to the operation of emissions trading are raised by the Commission. The Government agrees with the Commission that the development of a Community-wide pilot scheme is a necessary prelude to full international emissions trading and will actively participate in the development and implementation of the scheme.

Future Decisions on Trading

In light of the decisions at international level on the principles, modalities, rules and guidelines for the flexible mechanisms and the experience gained by the EU in any pilot scheme, the necessary decisions will be taken at national level and legislative underpinning put in place for domestic and international emissions trading. The Emissions Trading Advisory Group will be retained to assist as appropriate in these regards.

TAXATION OF GREENHOUSE GAS EMISSIONS

Taxation is of increasing prominence in action at EU level to address climate change and provides an economically efficient mechanism to assist early action. It also provides a direct signal of Government policy through the price mechanism and the most direct incentive for least cost action. Broad taxation instruments, rather than selective and specific controls and incentives, increase firms' scope for identifying the full range of responses that might be used in order to reduce emissions. They can be designed in a manner that ensures decision-makers are guided towards reducing emissions levels rather than opting for higher production costs, taking the place of compulsion and regulation in identifying changes that are cost-beneficial.

Integration with Overall Economic and Taxation Policy

Policy in relation to taxation is guided by the following considerations: -

▸ maintenance of the **stable economic environment and fiscal policies** which are necessary to support economic growth, enterprise promotion and international competitiveness;

▸ development of policies in a **social partnership** context, with a consensus on the need for prudent economic and fiscal policies, wage levels and targeted tax reductions to bring about tangible improvements in living standards, and tackle social exclusion, including with improved social

services;

▸ securing **low inflation** and **economic and employment growth** in the context of the *Stability Programme* to ensure compliance with the EU Stability and Growth Pact;

▸ maintaining budget positions in balance or in surplus in normal economic circumstances, and running significant **budget surpluses**, leading to continuing reductions in the **General Government debt**; and

▸ taxation reforms and changes to enhance **work incentives**, particularly for the lower paid, address **unemployment** and **poverty traps** increasing the effective **labour supply**, to promote **greater equity** and to improve the **interaction between the tax and social welfare systems.**

These overall considerations are of prime national importance and the introduction of greenhouse gas taxation will be undertaken in a manner compatible with them.

Introduction of Greenhouse Gas Emissions Taxation

In the context of acceptance by the social partners of taxation as one of the mechanisms to be used to meet our Kyoto target, Government will put in place an appropriate framework for greenhouse gas taxation, prioritising CO_2 emissions, from 2002 on a phased, incremental basis and in a manner that takes account of national economic, social and environmental objectives.

The Government's approach: -

▸ allows for **advance notice**, providing a signal to economic actors well ahead of the impact of the increasing levels of taxation;

▸ provides **policy certainty** for industry and economic actors;

▸ meets the **economic requirement** for decisions on planned investment to be taken in a rational and efficient manner;

▸ will ensure **avoidance of disruptions** and minimise impacts on the **Consumer Price Index (CPI)** by increasing taxes in a planned and predicted manner;

▸ will incorporate overall **tax recycling**; and

▸ will identify and remove any **subsidies** supporting inefficient use of energy.

Tax as an Instrument of Equity

A tax system applied across the economy as a whole provides a direct mechanism for ensuring equity between sectors in meeting Ireland's commitments. Such an approach also assists in identifying significant levels of "hidden" reductions of emissions in the economy, not all of which would be identified as efficiently and completely by other mechanisms, such as regulations, voluntary agreements, or "command and control" systems. The Government recognises that treatment of sectors within a tax regime should not affect the overall effort to secure sectoral equity or place an unfair burden on specific sectors, and will ensure that this does not occur.

Least Cost

The development of a broad greenhouse gas taxation regime, across all relevant sectors and gases, will assist in ensuring identification of the least cost approach for the economy as a whole in meeting our commitments. While economic instruments (including taxation) will be complementary to other instruments where these are more appropriate, an efficient taxation system helps reduce Government intervention by way of regulation, incentives etc., all of which impose costs on the Exchequer and within the economy.

International Competition

There is a need to balance the benefits of greenhouse gas taxation with any possible impact on the competitiveness of high greenhouse gas emitters which are also exposed to external competition from firms not paying comparable levels of tax. When recycling revenues it is intended that such sectors, while required to pay the full level of the tax, will be eligible for partial rebates having regard to EU Single Market and State Aid requirements and the provisions of the EU Excise Duty Directive when enacted. It is not intended to fully insulate these firms or sectors from the impacts of taxation, as this would eliminate the need to reduce levels of emissions and shift a greater burden onto other sectors of the economy.

Rebate, allowance, tax reduction, etc. schemes will be carefully designed to avoid/minimise distortions to competitiveness, whilst ensuring that the environmental dividend is secured. They will be continuously assessed against the evolution of comparable tax schemes in competitor economies.

Design Considerations

The Government is committed to a soundly based approach to greenhouse gas taxation so that both sustainable economic growth and achievement of the national greenhouse gas emissions limitations target are supported. Detailed analytical preparation and evaluation prior to the introduction of taxation measures will be overseen by the Tax Strategy Group. There are a range of design considerations for the introduction, and structure, of taxation measures: -

- ▶ **Revenue Recycling:** - so that measures are broadly fiscally neutral, provide new incentives (e.g. towards energy efficiency, reduce labour costs and enhance employment

protection) and disincentives (e.g. on energy inefficiency), ease the impacts on firms most affected (e.g. those using high levels of energy in sectors open to international competition) and on society (e.g. by minimising CPI effects); and promote social inclusion (e.g. those outside the wage system and/or dependent on welfare payments). Potential mechanisms include reductions in direct taxation, labour costs, PRSI, incentives for spending on energy efficiency, R&D, information and education programmes, reductions in rates of tax in the light of commitments made to quantified emissions reductions to be achieved at a sectoral level through negotiated agreements, etc. However, revenue recycling will **not** be used to insulate the sectors and firms concerned from the requirement to achieve sufficiently ambitious greenhouse gas emissions reductions.

- ▶ **Alternatives for Firms:** - so that decision-makers are guided towards reducing environmental impacts rather than opting for higher production costs, it will be necessary to assist in the identification and promotion of alternatives, such that taxation accelerates a shift towards the most environmentally beneficial behaviour. Relevant education, incentives and, where required, disincentives, to ensure change in the longer term will be provided (e.g. by the Irish Energy Centre (IEC) in relation to energy efficiency improvement options in industry).

- ▶ **Preventing Market Failure:** - The actors with most potential fully to acquire the information on the reduction potential are at the level of the firm. Where taxation of itself will not assist the owners and operators to do so fully (e.g. in the absence of necessary information and education programmes), support programmes designed to ensure the successful implementation of reduction programmes at firm level will be developed.

- ▶ **Levels of Tax:** - The maximum incentives to achieve the greatest marginal increase in efficiencies and reductions of emissions in a cost effective manner are required, and tax will be imposed at levels to maximise the emissions reductions response. Due regard will be had to the fact that elasticities vary from sector to sector.

- ▶ **Structure of Greenhouse Gas Emissions Tax:** - The structure of tax and exemptions/rebates is critical to maximising emissions reductions. The Government will determine the tax structure to maximise the benefits for low levels of emissions. Employment costs represent a significantly higher proportion of industry turnover than energy costs at a national level, and restructuring should have a positive impact on employment costs for most firms and sectors. It will also make a small, but important, improvement in the balance of payments, as most fossil fuel energy is imported.

- **Point of Taxation:** - The most efficient mechanism is to apply an "upstream" tax (on greenhouse gas emissions inputs), charged on the basis of the carbon equivalent content of fuel inputs in the case of energy production, greenhouse gas emissions from processes and the use of the industrial gases in the case of industry. This approach would provide particular incentives for renewable energy, which would not be taxed, as it has no carbon input. A pure "upstream" tax could have a disproportionate impact on security of energy supply, as fuel switching beyond an appropriate level may be brought about. Furthermore, in certain respects the EU proposals on excise duties would tax some forms of energy on a "downstream" basis. Accordingly, downstream taxation will also be applied, principally in the case of electricity consumption, without imposing double taxation. Balancing of tax between upstream and downstream taxes (on consumption) will be kept under review to ensure that no perverse incentives arise, such as inappropriate switching to electricity where use of other primary sources would lead to lower greenhouse gas emissions overall.

- **Review of Rates and Structures of Tax**: - The effectiveness and efficiency of taxation measures will be kept under continuous review; adjustments in the level of tax, or annual increases in tax, will be announced by Government in advance.

- **Relationship with Other Instruments:** - Taxation will be designed to reinforce and complement the benefits of improved regulation and standards, measures to address market failures and action to influence consumer behaviour. All such instruments and measures should be mutually reinforcing, with priority given to those that are most economically and environmentally efficient. Where reductions are made to tax levels arising from negotiated agreements, they will only be provided to the extent that the negotiated agreement reflects and delivers best international practice in the sector concerned. In this regard, negotiations will be undertaken on the range of agreements identified in this Strategy in step with the detailed development of specific taxation proposals.

- **Relationship with Emissions Trading:** - This will be reviewed in the context of finalising trading regimes. The review will include the identification of the extent of early action (for the purposes of taking account of such action in the allocation of emissions credits to firms) accruing from greenhouse gas emissions taxes.

Considerations for Individual Sectors

- In the **Energy** sector taxation will provide an incentive towards investments in energy or fuel efficiencies or investments in new, low- or no-carbon energy sources. It is necessary, on a long-term basis, beyond the first commitment period, that improvements and efficiencies are incorporated progressively into the Irish economy, already at one of the highest levels of per capita emissions in the developed world.

- For **Transport**, taxes on fuels are already a proxy for greenhouse gas taxes. While improvements have been introduced by the industry in relation to the fuel efficiency of individual vehicles, and further improvements are promised, setting taxes at appropriate levels should assist in controlling rapidly growing CO_2 emissions. Policy in relation to taxation of transport fuels is set out in Chapter 5.

- In the case of energy recovery from **Waste**, account will be taken of the offset of CH_4 and CO_2 emissions via the recovery of the energy from this source. As a further incentive to maximise energy recovery from this sector (displacing the production of energy from fossil fuel combustion in the main), unrecovered CH_4 emissions from landfill will be taxed as for process emissions from industry.

Chapter 4
Energy Supply

EMISSIONS/PROJECTIONS FOR ENERGY SECTOR

The energy supply sector contributed 32.0% of Ireland's CO_2 emissions and 21.6% of the basket of the three main greenhouse gases in 1990. Total electrical output is expected to almost double from 1995 to 2010, reflecting economic growth. However this is not expected to result in a parallel increase in CO_2 emissions, as international experience indicates that a shift in generation mix towards gas and CHP, which are less carbon intensive than the current fuel mix, and to renewables which are carbon neutral, can be expected. Overall, by 2010 emissions from this sector are expected to have grown by 62% above 1990 rates.

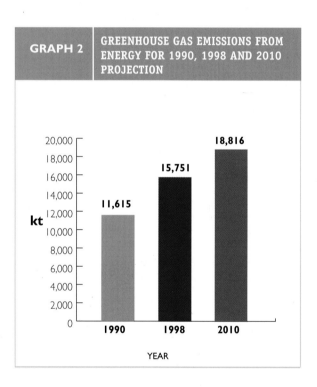

GRAPH 2	GREENHOUSE GAS EMISSIONS FROM ENERGY FOR 1990, 1998 AND 2010 PROJECTION

The energy supply sector contributes to CO_2 emissions through fossil fuel combustion almost exclusively; there are small (and reducing) emissions of CH_4 from pipeline leakages in the transmission of gas, and some N_2O formed in fuel combustion, with amounts arising being stabilised through the use of low-NOx burners in power generation.

MEASURES TO CONTROL GREENHOUSE GAS EMISSIONS

Two key sector-specific domestic policy options exist: -

▶ fuel switching, i.e. towards less carbon intensive fuels without affecting overall levels of electricity generation or use; and
▶ improving the efficiency of energy transformation.

These will be developed both on a sectoral basis and by the application of cross-sectoral instruments, in particular greenhouse gas taxation and emissions trading. Further analysis of these measures in respect of this sector will have regard to the relationship between energy supply, including electricity, and economic output.

Fuel Switching

Substituting for Coal

Fuel switching from coal has already contributed significantly to reduced greenhouse gas emissions in other countries and is expected also to be an important factor for many countries in meeting their Kyoto targets. Fuel switching to gas and to renewables for electricity generation will be supported by this Strategy. The development of electricity and gas interconnectors, (East/West and North/South as appropriate), will assist in addressing the security of supply issue and offer opportunities to access additional energy sources with reduced greenhouse gas emissions. Continuing support will be given to the exploration for indigenous supplies of gas, and appropriate arrangements made for its early recovery and exploitation.

Closure of Moneypoint with required new capacity provided by modern combined cycle gas turbine (CCGT) plant would make the largest single contribution to reduce greenhouse gas emissions (3.4 Mt CO_2 per annum). It is the Government's intention to ensure that measures addressing the energy supply sector, including emissions trading, greenhouse gas taxation and market liberalisation will be supportive of the ceasing of coal firing at Moneypoint by 2008 and a switch to greater use of gas and renewables. The factors which will support and accelerate this change include: -

▶ the scale of investment needed to refurbish Moneypoint, which will have been in service for over 20 years by 2008;

and

- the likely need for investment in flue gas desulphurisation (FGD) or other techniques (including low sulphur coal and/or reduced output), and Selective Catalytic Reduction (SCR) to reduce emissions of sulphur dioxide (SO_2) and nitrogen oxides (NOx) respectively from the plant to meet obligations for transboundary acidifying emissions. The capital costs of these technologies are of the order of £200m plus, with additional operating costs of some £20m per annum.

Closure of Moneypoint will increase dependence on gas for electricity generation to around 80% and in such circumstances it will be necessary to ensure the security of energy and electricity supply in the conversion of the plant output to gas. It will also require continuing intensification of the move to renewable energy and energy efficiency.

Substituting for Peat

Peat is the least carbon-efficient fossil fuel and will suffer significant additional cost disadvantages with the introduction of emissions trading and carbon/energy taxation, and the removal of environmentally perverse subsidies. To the extent that peat continues to be used for power generation, its use will become more efficient with the commissioning of the new Clonbullogue plant in 2001, and the construction of two further new plants which will progressively replace all remaining, low efficiency, peat generation. These new plants will use the minimum amount of peat compatible with economic operation within the Public Service Obligation (PSO), and their construction, operation and management will be benchmarked on best industry practice to maximise the efficient use of peat. In the context of this Strategy, best environmental practice will include ongoing assessment of greenhouse gas emissions.

Substituting for Oil

Following coal and peat, oil is the next most carbon intensive fuel. The liberalisation of energy markets is providing a commercial incentive for the replacement of some of the less efficient plants with gas, with an associated climate change gain.

CHP Expansion

Many large and medium scale energy users are actively looking at the options to maximise their returns from energy consumption by selling electricity as a by-product of heat generation. The efficiency of fuel utilisation is in excess of 80% in CHP plant run at optimum heat and electricity utilisation, compared to less than 40% in the most efficient alternative non-CCGT thermal generating plant. The existence of a significant heat requirement is essential to maximise the efficiency gains; without a suitable heat sink, the efficiency gains and associated greenhouse gas emissions reductions rapidly diminish. It is the intention, through the use of economic instruments and sustainable energy policy, to maximise the generation of electricity from this source, where the environmental gains can be fully demonstrated. £4m has been allocated in the NDP for the encouragement of high efficiency CHP, and the IEC has been asked to report on the future potential for CHP in the light of market liberalisation, technology advances, fuel sources, extension of the gas grid and financial incentives.

Renewables Expansion

The *Green Paper on Sustainable Energy* sets an ambitious target of doubling the proportion of the Total Primary Energy Requirement (TPER) to be generated from renewable resources in 2005, resulting from a planned trebling of the existing target for electricity from renewable sources, mainly wind. 500 MW_e additional electricity generating capacity is planned to be installed in the period 2000 – 2005, with an ongoing review of this in the light of experience, technological developments and Kyoto requirements. This will double the amount of electricity produced from renewable resources from 6.1% in 1998 to 12.4% in 2005. However, significant further expansion will be required if Ireland is to make a meaningful contribution to the EU target of 12% of TPER from renewables by 2010. At this stage 2% of Irish TPER is met from renewables, rising to 3.75% by 2005 under present targets.

The maximisation of renewables capacity is essential towards meeting our Kyoto Protocol target, and progress in attaining the targets for the increase in renewable capacity will be an important aspect of the biennial review of this Strategy. Additional targets will be set for 2005 – 2010, having regard, inter alia, to targets at EU level. The cost of renewable energy compared with the cost of energy derived from fossil fuels will fall with the introduction of carbon/energy taxes and the emissions trading system, under both of which renewable energies would not suffer any price impact. The market for renewable energy is being improved further by the development of a market for "Green Electricity", open to all purchasers of electricity, who will be able to purchase electricity which is produced using renewable forms of energy as its primary source. The work of the Renewable Energy Strategy Group in its recently published report *Strategy for Intensifying Wind Energy Development* dealing with the electricity market, the electricity network and spatial planning will be critical in ensuring the expansion of wind energy projects.

Gas Supply and Network Expansion

Gas can displace more carbon intensive energy fossil fuels,

particularly in relation to space heating in all sectors and process heating etc. in industry. The extension and strengthening of the existing gas network is under way and will continue to be encouraged as far as practicable to additional cities and towns, both under the existing monopoly distribution system and as the gas market is opened to competition.

Demand in natural gas has grown due primarily to the growth in the economy and the increase in demand for natural gas for the purpose of electricity generation. With the introduction of competition in the electricity market, demand for capacity in the natural gas network from prospective power producers exceeds capacity currently available in the network. The Gas (Amendment) Act, 2000 provides for a scheme to allocate a specific amount of capacity in the network for the purpose of fuelling new electricity generating capacity.

It is expected that additional capacity will be available by 2004, and will support necessary measures to promote fuel switching. There are already a number of parties interested in providing the necessary infrastructure to meet existing and future demands for natural gas. Bord Gáis Éireann and private parties can provide this infrastructure within the framework of existing legislation.

The energy sector investment, together with the sourcing of additional gas supplies and the strengthening of access to Trans European Energy Networks, is a vital supporting element of the Strategy, and progress will be reviewed regularly.

Other Pollutants

The Strategy will complement action to reduce emissions of other atmospheric pollutants including SO_2 and NOx. National emissions ceilings for these pollutants, as well as volatile organic compounds (VOCs) and ammonia (NH_3) have been set under the Gothenburg Protocol to address significant transboundary air pollution problems, including acidification, eutrophication and ground level ozone in an integrated manner. Additional proposals are being developed at EU level, and will require large reductions of emissions in the same timeframe as the Kyoto commitments. Electricity generation is a significant source of these pollutants, particularly SO_2, and a large source of NOx; in implementing the Strategy the Government will ensure that both climate change and transboundary air pollution requirements will be met in the most economically balanced manner.

Improving Generating Efficiency

In addition to its other duties, including the duty to promote competition in the generation and supply of electricity in accordance with the Electricity Regulation Act, 1999, the Commission for Electricity Regulation (CER) has a duty to take account of the protection of the environment and encourage the efficient use of electricity. The CER also has a duty to encourage research and development into methods of generating electricity using renewable, sustainable and alternative forms of energy and CHP, and into methods of increasing efficiency in the use and production of electricity. The discharge of these duties by the CER, together with the application by the EPA of Integrated Pollution Control (IPC) licensing to all existing and new plant (above 50MW) will require that energy is used efficiently in the generation of electricity and that all appropriate preventive measures are taken against pollution, in particular through application of Best Available Techniques (BAT).

Optimising burners to minimise the fuel input for maximum power output can achieve improving efficiency of electricity generation. The commercial incentive to improve efficiency rates will be assisted by market liberalisation within the overall remit of the CER, the Transmission System Operator (TSO), carbon/energy tax and emissions trading. The optimisation of CO_2 efficiency will be coordinated with the installation and operation of any necessary technologies to reduce emissions of SO_2 and NOx, which have a recognised impact on overall plant efficiency.

Demand Side Management (DSM)

The liberalisation of the electricity and gas markets has reduced the incentive that existed for a single supplier (the ESB) to promote DSM. An enhanced DSM programme will be integrated into the IEC as part of an intensified energy conservation/efficiency programme, with the cost to be supported by all players in the energy supply market.

TARGETS FOR THE ENERGY SUPPLY SECTOR

Indicative sectoral targets below business as usual for 2010 are: -

Fuel switching to gas	4.15 Mt CO_2
Moneypoint	*3.4 Mt CO_2*
Oil	*0.75 Mt CO_2*
CHP	0.25 Mt CO_2
Renewables	1.0 Mt CO_2
Efficiencies	0.1 Mt CO_2
DSM	0.15 Mt CO_2
Total	**5.65 Mt CO_2 per annum**

The cost in 1998 prices of achieving these targets is of the order of **£35m per annum**. Much of the target will be driven by the use of economic instruments, and the opportunities in the first instance for engaging in international emissions trading will be maximised to the extent possible for the sector to ensure that the least cost opportunities are identified.

36

Chapter 5
Transport

EMISSIONS/PROJECTIONS FOR TRANSPORT SECTOR

Transport is generally proving to be the most difficult sector in which to achieve controls on greenhouse gas emissions in most countries. In Ireland, roads are the dominant mode of internal transport, accounting for 90% of freight traffic and 96% of passenger traffic with public transport taking a decreasing proportion of the total transport market. Substantial traffic growth has taken place on the national road network over the past number of years (5% – 6% increase per annum), and there is a need to manage further anticipated growth in a manner consistent with environmental sustainability.

In Ireland, due to rapid economic growth, rapidly increasing levels of ownership and usage of private transport are evident. Ownership of cars is approaching the EU norm, from 230 per 1,000 head of population in 1990, to 317 in 1997 and a projected 430 by 2010. In addition, although fuel and emissions efficiencies within each class of car are increasing, there have been trends towards purchase of larger vehicles, reducing the overall fuel efficiency of the fleet. Transport sector greenhouse gases are, accordingly, set to grow further both in absolute terms and as a proportion of total greenhouse gas emissions.

At the end of 1998, there were 1.2 million private vehicles on Irish roads. These account for approximately 79% of all vehicles on the road. Some 171,000 freight, including approximately 15,000 heavy goods vehicles (HGVs), are also registered, representing 11% of all vehicles. There is not a linear relationship between the increase in vehicle numbers and total traffic volumes (private vehicle numbers are expected to increase by almost 75% between 1996 and 2010; the increase in travel kilometres undertaken is expected to increase by over 100% in the same period)[12], adding to the impact of the sector on greenhouse gas emissions. It is estimated that private vehicles contribute 60% of all transport sector greenhouse gas emissions and freight vehicles contribute 35%.

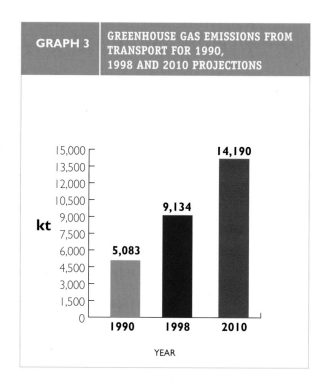

GRAPH 3 — GREENHOUSE GAS EMISSIONS FROM TRANSPORT FOR 1990, 1998 AND 2010 PROJECTIONS

In 1990, the transport sector contributed approximately 15.7% of Ireland's CO_2 emissions and 9.5% of base year greenhouse gas emissions. However, transport sector greenhouse gas emissions are forecast to increase by almost 180% in the period from 1990 to 2010. Transport sector emission increases are responsible for an estimated 59.1% of the total emissions increase to 2010, and the proportion of the total basket of greenhouse gas emissions the sector will be responsible for in 2010 is estimated at 18.9%, just double the proportion in 1990.

OECD and EU studies suggest that the environmental impact of road transport (air pollution, water, soil and land resources, congestion, noise, as well as impacts on neighbourhoods, habitats and landscapes) is up to 5% of GDP, with significant amounts of the overall costs (including infrastructural costs) not covered by revenues in the sector. This analysis does not include the external costs of climate change.

---

[12] External Evaluator Report 26 *Update of Forecasts of Vehicle Numbers and Traffic Volumes* (DKM Economic Consultants March 1998), and compatible with *Study of the Environmental Impact of Irish Transport Growth and of Related Sustainable Policies and Measures* (Oscar Faber December 1999). Volume 1 of the Oscar Faber Report is at http://www.irlgov.ie/tec/transport/report.htm

MEASURES TO CONTROL GREENHOUSE GAS EMISSIONS

No single policy measure is sufficient significantly to affect greenhouse gas emissions from transport. The range of policies to be applied should promote best environmental practices for all transport users, and inform their decisions towards the most greenhouse gas efficient options appropriate within national transport policy. However, in common with other countries, Ireland faces a difficult challenge in attaining sustainable transport and in particular limiting the growth in greenhouse gas emissions. Accordingly, a broadly based package of mutually reinforcing measures will tackle greenhouse gas emissions in the transport sector, and will be integrated both with one another and with complementary measures taken to achieve other policy priorities in the sector.

Sector specific actions for the transport sector are set out under the following headings: -
▸ Fuel Efficiency Measures;
▸ Modal Shift; and
▸ Demand Management.

Fuel Efficiency Measures

EU Agreement with Car Manufacturers
The voluntary agreement reached between the European Commission and European, Japanese and Korean car manufacturers will reduce CO_2 emissions from new cars by an average of 25% in the period from 1995 to 2008/2009. Across the EU, it is estimated that 15% of the necessary effort towards the overall climate change target of the EU will be met by this measure alone. Ireland will strongly support EU efforts towards setting more ambitious targets in the review of these targets in 2003, with the objective of achieving savings of up to 40% overall from the new car fleet by 2010/2012.

The higher than average expected growth in car numbers in Ireland and increased travel by the fleet counteract the national benefit of those measures, however; while action to promote the most efficient vehicles will help to maximise vehicle technology

benefits for Ireland, substantial additional measures are essential to address transport derived greenhouse gas emissions.

VRT and Annual Motor Tax
From a greenhouse gas perspective, it is not the ownership of cars *per se* that influences emissions, but the efficiency of the fleet and its utilisation. Vehicle Registration Tax (VRT) and annual motor tax are differentiated on the basis of engine size, which is an inexact proxy for levels of greenhouse gas and other emissions. The introduction in the coming years of new vehicle technologies through the EU Auto Oil programme (and the agreements with car manufacturers) will allow differentiation to a significantly greater degree than currently between CO_2-efficient and inefficient vehicles, including the promotion of alternative clean fuels. VRT and annual motor tax will be further rebalanced to favour the purchase of more fuel-efficient vehicles.

National Car Test (NCT)
Roadworthiness testing of private vehicles in the NCT will enhance environmental protection generally, including bringing about beneficial results in terms of fuel combustion, energy conservation and better consumer information on the mileage of used cars. The regular reports on the operation of the NCT will include reports on the average fuel efficiency of vehicles tested in the system, providing a basis for further analysis of the options for improving the fuel efficiency of the national vehicle fleet.

Fuel Economy Labelling
Ireland fully supports EU initiatives for fuel economy labelling of all new cars, and the monitoring of CO_2 emission rates for all newly registered cars. These will be implemented, preferably through a negotiated agreement with the Society of the Irish Motor Industry (SIMI), but if necessary through regulation by the Minister for the Environment and Local Government to ensure implementation by the due date. This will be supported through action by the Director of Consumer Affairs, the IEC and ENFO to improve public awareness of the cost, both financial and environmental, of purchaser choices.

Public Transport
Fuel switching towards the most CO_2 efficient alternatives to diesel will be encouraged in the public transport system. Reducing use of high sulphur diesel is necessary to improve air quality, particularly in urban areas where forthcoming EU ambient air quality standards will otherwise be difficult to meet. Adjustment of fuel taxation rebate rates will be used to promote the necessary shift.

Fleet Purchases

State and State agencies with large fleets will make progressive improvement in fuel efficiency in their fleets to ensure reductions in greenhouse gas emissions at 2% greater per annum than the average achieved nationally through the mix of measures listed above (agreements with manufacturers, VRT, fuel pricing).

Speed

Measures to reduce road accident rates and the unacceptably high levels of road deaths will mean reductions in excessive speeds, with resultant increases in fuel efficiency.

Modal Shift

Investment in and use of Public Transport

A total investment programme of £2.235bn in public transport improvements and upgrading is envisaged under the NDP. This has significant potential to reduce reliance on the private car for transport needs, especially in urban areas, with reductions in congestion and emissions, particularly in the Dublin area, and to secure more energy-efficient public transport, with consequential reductions in greenhouse gas and locally polluting emissions.

In the Greater Dublin area, the Economic and Social Infrastructure Operational Programme (ESIOP) will concentrate investment on the bus network, light rail, suburban rail, transport integration (park and ride, integrated ticketing, interchange facilities), cycle infrastructure and facilities, in addition to specific road improvement projects of particular relevance to the achievement of the DTI Strategy objectives.

Light Rail

£430m is being provided for the surface element of LUAS, with a contingency of £500m for the underground element. LUAS is expected to provide an extra 15% in suburban public transport capacity.

Suburban Rail

The short-term investment of £185m in DART and diesel rolling stock, as well as line upgrades and improvements, will increase DART capacity by 39% and suburban rail by 26%. Further options for future development are under evaluation. Decisions on further investment will be consistent with the land use development strategy as set out in the Strategic Planning Guidelines, and synergies will be ensured with the Development Plans of local authorities in the region. The evaluations and the development of synergies will be developed in the context of the

potential for the investment to make further contributions to reduce the rate of increase in greenhouse gas emissions.

Bus Services

Expansion of the bus network (including orbital and local routes), an additional 275 buses (a capacity increase of 28%), additional Quality Bus Corridors and fleet renewal will be supported by an investment of £220m.

Public Transport Integration

£50m is being provided, including an increase of 137% in the current programme for the provision of park and ride facilities, the development of facilities for intramodal and intermodal transfers, and integrated ticketing.

Traffic Management

To complement the measures supporting public transport, integrated traffic management and restraint schemes, such as those being undertaken by the Dublin Transportation Office (DTO), will be supported with an investment programme of £200m, including additional Quality Bus Corridors, further park and ride facilities, improved pedestrian facilities, development of the cycle network and improved traffic signalling and signposting.

Regional Public Transport

In addition to the investment in the Greater Dublin area, £650m is being made available for investment in regional public transport improvements, including mainline rail investment in safety and renewal (£500m), bus and rail improvements in the Greater Cork area, bus developments in Limerick, Galway and Waterford (£50m for the 4 cities), fleet replacement in Bus Éireann (£75m), regional bus improvements (£12m), and pilot measures for rural public transport to encourage local or community based initiatives to provide bus services in rural areas (£3.5m).

Roads Investment

As indicated, roads are the primary mode of internal transport in Ireland, and are vital for future economic and social development at both national and local level. Notwithstanding the high level of dependency on roads, the quality of the road infrastructure in Ireland is poor by EU standards; about 0.1% of the total road network is of motorway standard compared to an average of 1.3% in the EU. *The National Road Needs Study* (NRA, July 1998) pointed to the fact that by the end of 1999, 24% of the national primary network and 14% of the national secondary roads would fall below the required standard and that the position would worsen significantly by 2019 without additional significant investment.

The NDP aims to bring the road network up to an acceptable standard in the period to 2006 and to do so as part of an integrated transport investment programme.

Pursuant to this approach, a total of £4.7bn is planned in investment in National Roads in the NDP. On the National Primary network, a number of major interurban routes will be upgraded to motorway/high quality dual carriageway standard, with further major improvements on other national primary routes. On the National Secondary Network, the investment strategy will concentrate on routes which are of particular importance to economic and regional development. Within the primary road transport objectives is the objective to contribute to sustainable transport policies, facilitating continued economic growth and regional development while ensuring a high level of environmental protection. In the delivery of the investment programme, the assessment of environmental protection will include the assessment of the impact of individual projects on greenhouse gas emissions. The growth in these emissions will be managed through maximising the efficient use of road transport, removing delays in inter-urban journeys, (which, inter alia, will have the effect of increasing efficiencies in fuel use due to improved journey times and reduced congestion), road pricing, an integrated approach to land use planning and transport, including through the achievement of balanced regional development and the proposed National Spatial Strategy.

Freight

Improvements in the rail network through the increased investment in mainline rail will support improvements in freight operations and maximise modal switch to rail. The operational efficiency of road haulage (reduced "empty" running, use of air deflectors), improving greenhouse gas emissions efficiency of road haulage (optimising travel speeds, with benefits accruing also in relation to road safety and lower accident rates) must be increased. This will be achieved through awareness raising and education (including an expansion of the programmes of the IEC directed towards the sector, to be supported by the road haulage industry) and setting annual road taxes at appropriate levels, relating HGV taxation to, inter alia, fuel efficiency as well as axle weight. Any remaining barriers to the transport of freight by rail will be identified and removed.

In support of the increasing consumer requirement for modern logistics, just-in-time distribution and supply chain logistics, all of which require sustained investment in information technology by hauliers, the necessary training support will be directed to the sector by State agencies, with financing being provided by the sector. A strong emphasis will be maintained on limiting and reducing greenhouse gas emissions; in particular, any tendency for the evolution of freight practices, such as just-in-time distribution, to add to emissions will be addressed through a negotiated agreement between the Department of Public Enterprise and the road haulage industry. This agreement will include specific requirements on the industry to ensure that as freight policies evolve, the industry will actively adopt the most greenhouse gas emissions efficient options.

Demand Management

Increases in road transport and vehicle numbers have been closely tracking economic growth. It is widely recognised that improvements in infrastructure, public transport services and traffic management cannot cater for an indefinite increase in transport demand. Accordingly, demand management measures will be an increasingly important part of an integrated transport strategy to meet mobility needs in an environmental sustainable manner, both through management and restriction of demand and through effecting changes in modal choice.

Fuel Tax Measures

Measures will be taken to *limit* the rate of increase in overall fuel consumption and to encourage a switch to alternative cleaner and more CO_2 efficient fuels. Ireland has amongst the lowest prices for transport fuel in the EU, resulting in a significant distortion in the trade for fuels, including a perverse incentive for HGVs engaged in international transport to bunker in Ireland prior to travelling to elsewhere in the EU. These incentives did not exist in 1990, and fuel purchases attributable to this practice contributed an additional c. 0.6 Mt CO_2 to Ireland's 1998 inventory of emissions (rising to 0.9 Mt CO_2 in 1999), as the international practice is for the national sales of transport fuels to be used as the basis for calculating CO_2 emissions from the sector. Finding compensating reductions elsewhere in the economy may be an undue economic burden in the commitment period 2008 – 2012. It is intended progressively to reduce the incentive for foreign purchase of fuel in the State by 2008 by setting excise duty on transport fuel at appropriate levels.

It is recognised that inelasticities in demand, particularly in rural areas, may delay the achievement of reductions in domestic-related fuel use. Accordingly, movements in fuel taxes arising from this Strategy will be coordinated with the restructuring of VRT

and annual motor tax to ensure the maximum greenhouse gas emissions reductions effect whilst minimising the economic impact, particularly on rural communities.

Sustainable Transport

Within the framework established in *Sustainable Development: A Strategy for Ireland* (Department of the Environment 1997) it will be important to continue progressively to develop an integrated transport policy. In the Dublin region, where the most acute transport problems are to be found, DTO has revised and updated (October 2000) the Dublin Transportation Initiative (DTI) to take account of changed circumstances since its publication. The Update provides an overall planning framework for the development of the transport system for the Greater Dublin Area. Each project will have to be taken through a detailed planning process; this has already commenced for some projects. The DTI and the Update (with a time horizon to 2016) represent integrated transport initiatives dealing with all modes of surface transport as well as related issues such as traffic management and enforcement and are important elements of sustainable transport in the Dublin area.

A number of other major urban areas are also experiencing significant traffic congestion and a more integrated approach to transport planning is also being pursued in these areas through better integration of land use and transport planning; this aspect is dealt with in the following section.

Efforts will be continued and intensified to facilitate and develop a better integrated transport policy over the coming years.

Better Integration of Land Use and Transportation Planning

The principle that transport and land use planning are closely interconnected has long been acknowledged, but the practical alignment of land use and transport has proved difficult to attain. "Servicing" of development land has been largely understood to relate to water services, particularly drainage; generally speaking, a more stringent test has been applied by planning authorities to the availability of adequate water than of transport services.

This lack of full alignment between land use and transport policies has led to a number of problems. For example, extensive housing development has in the past been promoted in a number of urban areas which were poorly serviced locations for transport and which now suffer from peak hour traffic congestion. Equally, prevailing planning policies with relatively low housing densities did not facilitate access for public transport. Finally, even where good public transport access has been available, planning authorities

have not always responded consistently to optimise housing development potential or to promote employment intensive activities in such areas.

A number of initiatives are under way to address these shortcomings and to coordinate planning and transport issues more rationally. The premise for these initiatives is to provide for housing and other development needs in a way that does not exacerbate existing transport problems, that reduces the need to travel and facilitates, where feasible, the use of public transport. Land use and transportation studies are to be undertaken, updated or have been completed in Limerick, Waterford, Galway and Cork. Furthermore, for the first time, the 2000 provision for non-national roads includes funding for a new traffic management grants scheme in the cities of Cork, Galway, Limerick and Waterford, which will complement the scheme already in operation in the Dublin region. These schemes will help, inter alia, to promote more environmentally friendly ways of travelling and will help reduce congestion. The transport benefits of more integrated transport and land use planning will only be realised in the medium to long term.

The elements of policy to achieve better integration of land use and transportation planning include: -

Preparation of the National Spatial Strategy (NSS)

▸ The Strategy is being prepared over a two-year period as part of the Government's regional development policy, to reduce the disparities between and within regions and develop their potential to contribute to the continuing prosperity of the country.

▸ It will translate Government policy on balanced regional development into a more detailed blueprint for spatial development with a twenty-year perspective.

▸ The coordination of development strategies with transport needs assessment and the identification of spatial development patterns to contribute to efficient energy usage will be important elements of the NSS.

The consultation process for the preparation of the NSS will seek consensus on the measures contributing to the management of greenhouse gas emissions from transport.

Development of Regional Planning Guidelines (RPGs)

▸ These will provide a long-term strategic planning framework for development at the regional level.

▸ Population trends, locations for development, infrastructural needs such as transport, energy and the protection of the environment will be provided for.

▸ In making RPGs, a Regional Authority must have regard to proper planning and sustainable development, and Government policy, including this Strategy.

▸ The Strategic Planning Guidelines for the Greater Dublin Area provide for the consolidation of existing built-up areas with further development being located where it can be served by an enhanced public transport system.

▸ Planning authorities will have to ensure consistency with relevant RPGs when making and adopting development plans; following the making of guidelines, these plans must be reviewed, and varied if necessary.

Residential Density

▸ The planning guidelines on residential densities for housing development will improve the efficiency of public transport, promote cycling and walking as viable options and reduce demand for transport by car.

▸ They encourage more sustainable urban development through the avoidance of excessive suburbanisation and the promotion of higher residential densities favouring areas well served by public transport and in other appropriate locations in conjunction with improved public transport systems; increased densities facilitate viable public transport systems.

▸ Development plans will be revised to give full effect to the residential density guidelines and they will also be given effect in day-to-day planning operations.

Planning and Development Act, 2000

The purposes for which objectives may be indicated in a development plan include the following under the Act: -

▸ Promoting sustainable settlement and transportation strategies in all areas.

▸ Facilitating the provision of sustainable transport, public transport and road traffic systems and promoting the development of local transport plans.

Integrated Development Planning

The East and Mid-East Regional Authorities are developing an integrated development planning framework for the Greater Dublin Area, based on the principles of sustainable development and emphasising the use of public transport. This will necessitate co-operation and coordination with, inter alia, the NRA, DTO, Department of Public Enterprise, Dublin Bus, Bus Éireann, Iarnród Éireann and the relevant local authorities.

Retail Development Guidelines

Large-scale retail development largely dependent on private car transport from a wide catchment area adds to the growth in traffic volume and greenhouse gas emissions: -

▸ Draft retail planning guidelines addressing the complex planning issues around large-scale retail development, including outside existing urban areas, have been published.

▸ The guidelines provide for the promotion of retail development only in locations that are readily accessible, particularly by public transport, and encourage a preference for multi-purpose trips.

▸ Planning policy supports the continuing role of town and district centres and reinforcing investment in urban renewal, thus allowing national roads and motorways to fulfil their regional and national transport role.

Final Retail Planning Guidelines are expected to issue in 2000.

Vehicle Restraint

Improving public transport will be accompanied by restraints on vehicle use through increased parking controls and reallocation of road space. Exemption from benefit-in-kind taxation was introduced from 1999 for employees whose employers provide them with monthly/annual travel passes. A fair and workable system of benefit-in-kind taxation on commuter car-parking spaces is being developed by the Department of Finance and the Revenue Commissioners and will be introduced to encourage a switch from private car use to public transport.

Road Pricing

Elements of road pricing (e.g. tolling) are already in use, and a consultancy study has examined the contribution which more comprehensive use of this mechanism might make to effective traffic management in Dublin. The consultants concluded that road pricing could have a role to play in transport policy for Dublin; they also considered that the issue requires more detailed consideration in the context of an integrated approach to Dublin's transport requirements and that any future pricing initiative is likely to require balancing by a range of other measures. The consultants' report is being considered in the context of a demand management plan being prepared by the DTO. Climate change considerations will be integrated into this consideration to maximise climate change gains and additional improvements in urban air quality.

Use of IT to Reduce Transport

Information technology has the potential to reduce greenhouse gas emissions by reducing the use of transport. Teleworking opportunities will be encouraged with the development of options for teleworking within the public service and for its provision in the private sector.

Further development of e-commerce has the potential to reduce greenhouse gas emissions by reducing the use of transport.

Use of Telematics

The progressive use of advanced telematics in urban areas will help to reduce congestion and improve the efficiency of the transport system. Technology in the form of telematics and intelligent traffic management and signalling systems is also being harnessed to provide better use and logistical management of transport infrastructure, both road and rail. This will lead to a reduction in emissions of greenhouse gases.

TARGETS FOR THE TRANSPORT SECTOR

Indicative sectoral targets below business as usual for 2010 will be:-

Vehicle Efficiency Improvements	0.77 Mt CO_2
Fuel Measures (displace bunkering)	0.9 Mt CO_2
VRT, Taxes	0.5 Mt CO_2
Labelling	0.1 Mt CO_2
Public Transport Measures	0.15 Mt CO_2
Traffic Management	0.2 Mt CO_2
Freight	0.05 Mt CO_2
Total	**2.67 Mt CO_2 per annum**

The equivalent annual cost for these measures is approximately **£80m**. However, it should be noted that there is some degree of overlap between the measures; actual CO_2 savings will be monitored and estimates adjusted accordingly.

Chapter 6
**Built Environment
and Residential
Sector**

EMISSIONS/PROJECTIONS FOR BUILT ENVIRONMENT AND RESIDENTIAL SECTOR

Housing Sector

The residential sector is responsible for approximately 29% of CO_2 emissions (1998) and 20% of all greenhouse gas emissions, when emissions from electricity for the sector are included.

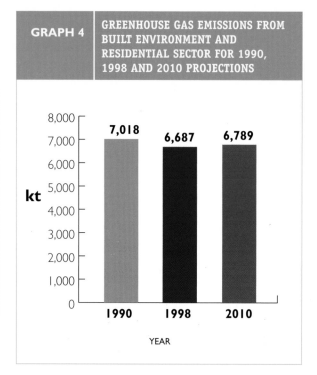

GRAPH 4	GREENHOUSE GAS EMISSIONS FROM BUILT ENVIRONMENT AND RESIDENTIAL SECTOR FOR 1990, 1998 AND 2010 PROJECTIONS

kt

1990	1998	2010
7,018	6,687	6,789

YEAR

Emissions of greenhouse gases attributable to the sector are almost exclusively CO_2, from energy use consumed domestically for space heating etc., and electricity consumed in domestic appliances. Small amounts of CH_4 and N_2O associated with fuel use are also emitted.

Commercial/Services Sector

Disaggregation of emissions within the sector to identify emissions specifically related to building use are not available, and overall emissions for the sector are dealt with in Chapter 7 dealing with the Industry, Commercial and Services Sector.

However, it is estimated that the provision of space heating and the use of appliances in all buildings accounts for approximately 40% of all energy use and hence almost the same proportion of national CO_2 emissions.

MEASURES TO CONTROL GREENHOUSE GAS EMISSIONS

There are five key ways in which emissions from this sector can be reduced: -

▶ improved spatial and energy use planning;
▶ better insulated and more energy efficient new buildings, including housing;
▶ improved energy efficiency of existing buildings, including housing;
▶ improved energy efficiency of domestic and other energy using appliances; and
▶ changing fuel mix to greater use of less CO_2 intensive fuels and renewable energy sources.

Improved Spatial And Energy Use Planning

Spatial Planning and Development

In addition to promoting efficiency in the use of energy, transport and natural resources, spatial planning and land use policies (including in particular the Local Government (Planning and Development) Act, 2000, the National Spatial Strategy and Regional Planning Guidelines) provide an essential framework towards maximising the use of already developed areas and determining the most appropriate locations for necessary new housing development.

▶ The **National Development Plan** provides the necessary investment strategy to facilitate the provision of an estimated 500,000 houses to address demand between 2000 and 2010. Recent projections of housing demand indicate that further significant increases in housing supply will be required over this timeframe to meet increased demand. Failure to address our housing needs effectively would impose significant costs and constraints upon Ireland's economic growth, competitiveness and social development;

▶ **Investment** in economic and social infrastructure such as public transport, roads, water, waste water and other services will be planned and integrated with housing provision to ensure more sustainable patterns of development.

New housing will, as far as possible, be provided sustainably by consolidating existing major urban areas and areas where communities are already established and where services such as public transport, shops, employment opportunities and schools exist and their utilisation can be maximised.

Residential Density Guidelines

Increasing the density of residential accommodation provides an opportunity to achieve a more economic and efficient use of existing infrastructure and serviced land, a reduced need for the development of "greenfield" sites, less urban sprawl and ribbon development, better integration with commercial centres, employment opportunities and public transport provision, leading to more sustainable commuting patterns. Guidelines, the implementation of which will be monitored by the Department of Environment and Local Government, have issued to local authorities towards achieving more sustainable practices. Planning authorities have been directed to review and vary their Development Plans to give full effect to the recommendations and policies contained in the Guidelines.

The DTO and public transport companies will make the necessary improvements and adjustments to public transport systems and infrastructure to facilitate vigorous implementation of the Guidelines.

Integrated Energy Planning

Increasing the density of residential accommodation, particularly in urban areas, and integration with commercial and other developments, also provides an opportunity to reflect energy planning considerations more explicitly in the provision of new housing. This can occur e.g. through the use of CHP plants for commercial/residential developments (where sufficient heat sinks are available to make this an environmentally suitable option) and the use of district heating (e.g. waste heat from power stations will be available in the Dublin Docklands redevelopment area). Tax and other incentives, including adjustments to the provisions of the urban renewal schemes, will be developed to encourage this approach, and barriers to development of high-efficiency CHP schemes (e.g. difficulties with access to the National Grid) will be removed.

The input from Local Energy Agencies (LEAs) will be of critical importance in developing local partnership based approaches on suitable programmes. LEAs have a significant potential in integrating energy and environmental policy through linking top-down policy with bottom-up consumer based practical initiatives. The Agencies, in partnership with local authorities and the IEC, will be tasked with identifying and promoting suitable programmes.

More Efficient New Buildings

Building Regulations

The improvements in building standards and energy efficiency in new housing made mandatory by the Building Regulations in 1991 led to a 20% reduction in energy use in new buildings. Revisions to the Building Regulations in 1997 contributed a further reduction of up to 10%. Scope remains for substantial further improvement through this mechanism. A review of Part L of the Regulations (Conservation of Energy and Fuel) is currently underway by the Department of Environment and Local Government in consultation with the Building Regulations Advisory Board (BRAB), and relevant sectors of the construction industry.

A reduction of energy use in new housing of the order of 20% will be targeted in revised Regulations in mid-2002, with a further significant improvement in 2005. The revision of the Regulations is contingent on the outcome of a study commissioned by BRAB on the impact of proposed higher insulation standards on building systems and the quality of indoor air climate (and thus on the health of the occupants).

Appropriate technical guidance and advice will be provided in a revised edition of Technical Guidance Document on the amended Building Regulations.

Sustainable and Energy Efficient Buildings

In the development of sustainable building guidelines and practices, full regard will be had to the greenhouse gas emissions reductions potential of their early incorporation into construction industry practice. Research and demonstration projects indicate that significant savings in energy use for space and water heating are achievable when appropriate building form, fabric and orientation (including passive and active solar heating, energy efficient heating and heat recovery systems) choices are made. In the context of social housing a number of initiatives have already been undertaken or are planned. A pilot energy efficient integrated social and private housing scheme was constructed in Dublin in 1999 with the assistance of the EU Thermie programme, as a demonstration model; this is now being evaluated in terms of its improved efficiency, cost effectiveness and possibilities for wider implementation in private and social housing construction. The Masterplan for the Regeneration of Ballymun envisages that some 5% of new houses will be innovative and some 1% experimental, with both innovation and experimentation concentrating on aspects of sustainability. Lessons learned from these and other similar initiatives will be applied to the social housing sector generally.

First Time Buyers' Grant

Government policy reflected in the *Green Paper on Sustainable Energy* has identified the possibility of restructuring the existing first time buyer grant so that larger grants will be available towards more efficient houses; this restructuring will be completed by 2002. This restructuring will require the identification of verifiable standards of improved energy efficiency as part of a package for promoting sustainable building practices. In addition, comparable restructuring in favour of more efficient housing will be put in place in the same timeframe in regard to the incentives and requirements in respect of housing in designated urban and rural areas. Suitable additional tax incentives or other market stimulation measures to promote uptake of these technologies will be developed.

Low Energy Housing

The Minister for the Environment and Local Government, in cooperation with the IEC, will develop a scheme of support for Demonstration Low Energy projects in all categories of housing. The aim will be to provide practical experience and information for designers, builders, purchasers and occupiers. The results will also inform future reviews of Building Regulations. This will be undertaken in the context of the RD&D proposals in the *Green Paper on Sustainable Energy.*

The revised guidelines on the design of social housing, published in 1999 and applicable to local authorities and voluntary housing bodies, place considerable emphasis for the first time on the need to ensure that individual housing schemes are environmentally sustainable. Issues such as micro-climate, ecology, choice of materials, day-lighting and solar gain and insulation are highlighted. Local authority housing is constructed to energy efficiency standards meeting or exceeding the 1997 Building Regulations. All social housing construction will meet improved standards imposed by the future amendments to the Building Regulations.

Replacement of Obsolescent Housing

The significantly increased rate of housebuilding activity, particularly since 1995, and the projected further significant increase in housing output to 2010, of which it is expected that a sixth will replace older more inefficient housing, will ensure that a very high proportion of the housing stock will meet the higher energy efficiency standards introduced in 1992. By the end of

2000, 25% of the housing stock will have been constructed since June 1992, and this will rise to over 50% of the housing stock by 2010. By 2010, over 40% of the housing stock will have been constructed post-1997 when revisions to the Building Regulations further improved energy efficiency standards. The units lost to the housing stock in the period through obsolescence etc. will predominantly be the older substandard housing with the poorest energy efficiency. Ireland, by 2010, will, by European standards, have a very modern housing stock constructed to high energy efficiency standards.

Improved Efficiency Of Existing Buildings

Reducing Energy Consumption in Existing Houses

Much of the existing housing stock continues to use energy in a relatively inefficient manner. In addition to relatively high levels of energy use, this also contributes to a significant problem of fuel poverty. Fuel poverty describes the condition of low-income households living in poorly insulated and inefficiently and inadequately heated housing, which experience poor heating standards while spending a relatively high proportion of their income on fuel. Improved thermal efficiency can contribute to both reduced energy consumption and more adequate levels of heating and has the potential to be both environmentally and socially beneficial.

Feasible options for improving energy efficiency in the remaining less energy efficient pre-1991 stock include: -

▸ insulation (hot water tank, loft, cavity wall, solid wall, timber and concrete floors);
▸ double-glazing or low-e glazing;
▸ draught-proofing;
▸ high efficiency boilers using fuels with lower emissions.

Many effective measures can be achieved at negative or zero equivalent annual cost to the householder[13]. However, insufficient numbers of householders are availing of the cost savings arising from these opportunities; some may not be aware of such energy-saving measures and some are not in a position to implement the more capital-intensive measures because they do not have sufficient funds to make the initial investments. Moreover, the households which would benefit most from the installation of more energy-efficient technologies are likely to find it more

---

[13] *Homes for the 21st Century* (prepared by Energy Research Group & Environmental Institute, UCD, and published February 2000 by Energy Action Ltd.) indicated the potential of a programme to improve the thermal efficiency of all existing houses to a standard approximating a typical new 1997 house, as far as practicable. A fully implemented programme over 10 years is estimated to give total emission reductions of the order of 3 Mt CO_2 at a cost of some £1.26bn. Discounting certain assumptions about desirable comfort and heating levels, and fuel switching, estimated emission reductions would be less (0.8Mt CO_2 or lower).

difficult to obtain such funds and likely to have more pressing priorities for extra funds.

The modernisation of the existing housing stock is progressed by a number of Government assisted schemes, operated by local authorities and the Health Boards to improve the housing conditions of those considered most at risk of **fuel poverty, local authority tenants** (80% of whom are social welfare dependant) and the **elderly**.

▸ Assistance for elderly home owners through the Essential Repairs Grants Schemes administered by local authorities (effective maximum grant increased to £6,000 in December 1999 and greater flexibility allowed in relation to the type of works which may be carried out) and the Task Force on Special Housing Aid for the Elderly, administered by the Health Boards (record funding of £8m being provided in 2000, making it possible to provide, more generally, heating systems which are appropriate to the needs of the elderly in the context of the other works to their homes).

▸ The Remedial Works Scheme, with significant resources, targets the improvement and upgrading of low cost, pre-1960 dwellings and run down local authority urban estates, including area-based regeneration initiatives to address comprehensively a number of run-down flat complexes. The upgrading of the social rented stock will improve the standard of accommodation and will result in more efficient heating systems and overall improved energy efficiency.

▸ The Commission on the Private Rented Residential Sector has recommended that the high level of non-compliance by landlords with the provisions of the Standards Regulations and the low level of enforcement activity by local authorities should be urgently addressed. It also strongly recommended that any tax incentives or reliefs being introduced on foot of its recommendations to promote investment and greater professionalism in the sector should be contingent on compliance with all regulatory controls. It is envisaged that these recommendations, along with the proposed introduction of a local authority rent assistance scheme for private rented accommodation to replace the existing Supplementary Welfare Allowance rent assistance scheme, will form the basis for a general improvement of standards in the private rented residential sector.

The refurbishment and upgrading of the existing housing stock is also assisted through the significant number of second-hand houses that are sold each year – over 50,000 (approx.). Many of these houses are substantially renovated and improved by their new owners.

The key requirements in ensuring a significant reduction in fuel poverty and the achievement of the available energy savings include:-

▸ narrowing the information gap;

▸ reducing the opportunity and transaction costs of investment in energy conservation;

▸ ensuring the availability of funds to those who need them most; and

▸ provision of the correct incentives (to landlords, tenants) to ensure investment.

Particular attention will also be paid to the development of suitable instruments to achieve the maximum emissions reductions in the existing private residential sector: -

▸ in addition to the impact of the introduction of economic instruments in the energy sector, educational and awareness programmes by the IEC will be intensified to promote penetration of these options and to fill the existing information gap for consumers and producers;

▸ the establishment of LEAs is being encouraged in all parts of the country; they will be tasked, in partnership with the IEC, local authorities and local business interests, with promoting action at local level; and

▸ the particular importance of Energy Action (because of the importance of its work in combating fuel poverty) will be further recognised and the Department of Public Enterprise will give priority attention to increasing its funding from 2001.

National House Condition Survey

National House Condition Surveys are carried out every ten years and the next survey will take place in 2001. The 2001 Survey will include, for the first time, an energy efficiency module which will provide information relating to type of heating, insulation and whether specific steps have been taken by households to improve energy efficiency in their homes. The data obtained will contribute significantly to the information currently available in respect of existing standards and provide a benchmark against which improvements over the period of this strategy can be measured in the 2011 House Condition Survey.

Energy Efficiency Rating

Pre-1991 houses, not subsequently adequately upgraded, generally do not meet modern standards for energy efficiency. A scheme to require the vendor to provide an energy efficiency certificate, from a competent contractor, showing the annual energy consumption (including cost) of the premises and the requirements necessary to reduce this consumption substantially, listed in efficiency and cost terms, will be established. This will be developed in a manner to ensure that the purchase and upgrading of old housing is not discouraged, particularly by first-time buyers. It would be a matter for the purchaser to compare house prices on the basis of this certificate and to determine energy efficiency investments to be made after purchase. The IEC will have responsibility for regulating the contractors providing the certification.

In the commercial sector, a mandatory energy rating system will be developed to promote greater awareness of the cost of energy as a portion of the overall costs of building rental. Adjustments to the tax treatment of leases will be made if it becomes clear by 2003 that the energy rating system is not providing the necessary incentive on its own to reduce energy use in the sector.

Refurbishment of Commercial Buildings

There is a higher turnover of commercial than of residential properties, most of which require refitting before re-use. The refit rate is also high without transfer of ownership. Firms will be encouraged to adopt ISO 14001 or EMAS requirements, enabling the use of energy in the enterprise to be addressed. Negotiated agreements will be developed, with the assistance of the IEC, with representative bodies in the sector to increase the rate of uptake of these instruments.

For both new and refurbished buildings, the focus will be on management of heating, ventilation and natural lighting gain to enable natural and adventitious heating to be used to a maximum, and to facilitate non-mechanical ventilation and a reduction of lighting requirements.

Improved Energy Efficiency Of Appliances

Appliance Efficiencies

Improvements in the energy efficiency of appliances can be made in respect of: -

▸ condensing boilers;
▸ low energy lights;
▸ efficient appliances (dishwashers, refrigerators, freezers, fridge/freezers, cookers, washing machines, tumble dryers, TVs, kettles).

Ireland is generally a technology taker in the white goods sector, dependent on action at EU or wider international levels to improve labelling standards, as currently applying to all fridges,

freezers and washing machines. Ireland will strongly support the extension of mandatory labelling to all relevant appliances. As described in Chapter 7, a negotiated agreement will be developed with retailers of such goods to encourage the sale of the more efficient appliances, with appropriate targets for performance. The IEC will develop the necessary education and promotion programmes, in partnership with the retailers, to support this negotiated agreement.

Fittings in Commercial Buildings

Many fittings can be altered during refurbishment or included in construction; however, significant energy savings can be made independently of major refits. These focus on installing energy efficient equipment through "green purchasing" policies, including lighting, heating and appliances. With the assistance of the IEC, a negotiated agreement will be developed with the representative organisations for the sector to develop such policies.

Demand Side Management (DSM)

In the residential and commercial sectors, DSM has potential to improve electricity generating efficiencies, through night running of appliances, etc. The IEC will develop, with all providers of electricity in the liberalised market, a tailored programme to continue DSM in these sectors. (See also Chapter 4).

Changing Fuel Mix

Emissions can also be reduced by changing the fuels which are used for space heating. Most scope for switching to gas lies with households and enterprises which actually have gas in their neighbourhood but are not connected to the gas supply, particularly those which use solid fuel for space heating. Bord Gáis will develop programmes to maximise the use of gas in households and other buildings. The Residential Density Guidelines, with the emphasis on development in existing areas rather than greenfield sites, will assist in enabling the extension of the gas network to the greatest number of new houses and other buildings.

Electricity derived from fossil fuels used for space heating is an inherently inefficient use of electricity due to the loss of energy at generation and in transmission (at most, only 45% efficiency in the use of fossil fuel energy input is achievable at final consumption). Accordingly, measures (including awareness programmes by the IEC and gas utility, and if required, differentiated taxation measures) will be developed to discourage this use of electricity where the gas network (70% to 80% efficiency achievable) is available. Emissions do not arise where this electricity is produced from renewable sources; the disincentives developed to inhibit the use of electricity for space heating will take account of this. The energy utilities will be obliged, through negotiated agreement if possible, to make the necessary adjustments to their tariff rates to ensure efficient use of fuels.

FURTHER MEASURES

State Organisations

The State must provide a lead in reducing energy use and greenhouse gas emissions in buildings under its control. In State and semi-State organisations, arrangements for environmental audit, including energy use, will be accelerated. This will include an expansion of the scheme between the IEC and the OPW to collect data on energy uses and efficiencies; this will be accompanied by the application of sufficient human and other resources at the level of the individual unit to ensure that the available savings (including expenditure savings), are achieved. Refurbishment work will provide a particular opportunity to maximise savings, especially long-term savings. Incentives will be developed, through the multi-annual budgetary process to ensure that individual offices and Departments have sufficient incentive to seek and implement available savings.

The target is for each unit to be benchmarked against best international practice for each type of building (e.g. naturally ventilated, air conditioned, etc.) by 2002, and to achieve the energy savings by 2005.

Awareness Raising and the Provision of Information

It is clear from many of the measures outlined above that a coordinated approach to the provision of information and awareness campaigns will be required, and that information and awareness will be particularly important tools in the **residential sector.** This coordination will be ensured by the IEC with the assistance of LEAs, working in partnership with all energy suppliers, local authorities and ENFO.

In the **commercial sector,** economic instruments provide a mechanism to encourage improvements in practices and efficiencies. However, given the diversity of the sector and the small size of many players, these need to be supported by ongoing awareness and promotion campaigns. These will be intensified and be the responsibility of the IEC. The IEC will also identify the energy efficiency training needs of the sector, and negotiate with educational institutions (both commercial and State supported) for the provision of the necessary facilities, the upgrading of existing courses etc. and the identification of the incentives required for the encouragement of the training of existing staff within firms.

TARGETS FOR THE BUILT ENVIRONMENT AND RESIDENTIAL SECTOR

Spatial Planning Practices

Because of the long lead-time for direct results, no targets are set for the initial commitment period under this heading, although it has an important contribution to make to achieving savings in e.g. the transport sector, and to position Ireland for the purposes of future commitment periods. Particular importance will attach to the completion of the National Spatial Strategy within 2 years.

Building Regulation	0.25 Mt CO_2, plus additional savings from further improvements in Building Regulations in 2005.
Existing Buildings	0.4 Mt CO_2 in energy efficiency measures.
Fuel Mix	0.25 Mt CO_2
Total	**0.9 Mt CO_2 per annum**

The estimated cost is **£25 – £33m** per annum.

Chapter 7
Industry, Commercial and Services Sector

EMISSIONS/PROJECTIONS FOR INDUSTRY AND COMMERCIAL SECTORS

The Irish economy has enjoyed rapid growth in recent years, which, has helped to greatly expand overall productive capacity. Industry in Ireland currently accounts for 27% of total employment and 38% of GDP. The industrial sector mainly contributes to greenhouse gas emissions through energy use including direct consumption of fossil fuels and use of electricity, and through direct emissions from a number of industrial processes – for example, cement manufacture (energy and process) which accounted for 2.8% of total CO_2 equivalent emissions in 1990, is projected to rise to 8% of gross emissions in 2010.

Manufacturing Industry

Emissions of greenhouse gases from manufacturing industry, including emissions as by-products of manufacturing processes (e.g. cement), accounted for 13.5% of emissions in 1990. Emissions associated with electricity production consumed by this sector were additional. Business as usual projections indicate that emissions from manufacturing industry will increase by 5.4 Mt CO_2 equivalent in the period from 1990 to the commitment period of 2008 – 2012.

The industrial sector is also the primary source of emissions of the **industrial gases.** Because of their use in the electronics sector, and the use of HFC as a replacement for CFCs in essential medical uses, growth in the emissions of these gases is expected to be exceptionally strong. Potential emissions will increase by 635%[14], albeit from a very low base, on the basis of available data. This is similar to the increases expected in some other countries, but many will have a significantly lower rate of increase.

Commercial/Services

The remainder of the sector (commercial, small firms, services) is responsible for approximately 3.3% of greenhouse gas emissions, arising from energy consumption, in addition to electricity consumption by the sector. The services (non-traded) sector accounts for over 50% of total GDP. Much of its output is an intermediate input into the industrial sector, for example through personal services, consultancy, and financial services, but it also includes offices, entertainment, tourism and leisure facilities, shops, retail and warehouses, and public services and amenities. Arising from increased automation, air conditioning, etc., electricity consumption by the commercial sector is expected to grow rapidly.

There are no significant emissions of any gas except CO_2 from the commercial and services part of the sector.

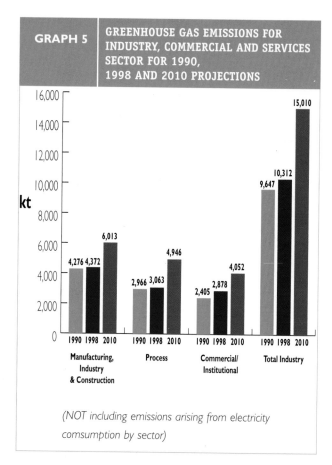

GRAPH 5	GREENHOUSE GAS EMISSIONS FOR INDUSTRY, COMMERCIAL AND SERVICES SECTOR FOR 1990, 1998 AND 2010 PROJECTIONS

(NOT including emissions arising from electricity comsumption by sector)

A 1995 base year is used for the industrial gases in this and all other graphs in the Strategy

---

[14] The inventory of industrial gases is incomplete and is being developed by the EPA. The increase on the basis of "actual emissions" is projected at 160%. See also Appendix 2.

MEASURES TO CONTROL GREENHOUSE GAS EMISSIONS

The **key instruments** to be applied in this sector will be: -

▸ **Investment Analysis:** - All industrial development agencies, coordinated and supervised by the Department of Enterprise, Trade and Employment, will examine inward and indigenous investment proposals and opportunities from the perspective of impact on greenhouse gas emissions. Where potential emissions would have a disproportionate impact on national emissions and the achievement of the Kyoto target (especially where emissions are expected to be greater than the norm for the sector concerned), the cost to the economy of achieving compensatory savings elsewhere will be part of the overall assessment of the proposal. The treatment of potential JI projects based in Ireland is dealt with in Chapter 3.

▸ **Regulation**: - IPPC licensing will require the adoption of Best Available Techniques (BAT) for energy use and control of greenhouse gas emissions. Where trading or negotiated agreements are operated on a sectoral basis, a sectoral "bubble" agreement developed in accordance with the "general binding rules" provision of the IPPC Directive (article 9.8 of Directive 96/61/EC) will be adapted to optimise the costs of achieving the reductions required by BAT.

▸ **Taxation**: - This will be a significant instrument in this sector. Within the sector, it will be applied to all appropriate forms of production, in accordance with the guiding principles set out in Chapter 2 and the considerations in Chapter 3.

In the case of sectoral negotiated agreements, taxation will remain a key option to tackle "free riders" and lack of progress in the effective implementation of negotiated agreements. It will also be used as a supplementary instrument where the other instruments cannot optimise greenhouse gas reduction potentials.

▸ **Negotiated Agreements:** - These are a key component of the partnership approach to economic development. As significant action will be needed to achieve our Kyoto target, targets for all negotiated agreements put in place pursuant to this Strategy must be significantly beyond business as usual

scenarios. The Government also endorses the view of the EU Council of Environment Ministers which recognised that "environmental agreements must have specified objectives, be transparent, reliable and enforceable" in order to be effective. This will be vital to the credibility of any agreement. As provided for in Chapter 3, offsetting efficiency gains against reductions to tax levels arising from negotiated agreements will only be provided for to the extent that the reductions arising from the negotiated agreement are comparable to those achieved through best international practice.

▸ **Emissions Trading:** - through which economic efficiencies in greenhouse gas reductions can be rewarded and least cost options maximised. The considerations set out in Chapter 3 will apply.

In the first two key instruments identified above, ongoing review is implicit in the operation of investment analysis and the application of IPPC licensing by the agencies concerned and the EPA. In the case of the application of taxation and the development of negotiated agreements, sector-level implementation and review mechanisms will be established at the appropriate Departmental level. The overall implementation and review mechanisms for the Strategy, as set out in Chapter 11, will oversee and report on implementation at sectoral level.

KEY ACTIONS

Sector specific actions will include the following: -

Energy Efficiency Improvements

Negotiated Agreements with Industry

The IEC has identified a range of priority technologies and measures for achieving energy efficiency gains within industry. Many are low cost or have cost benefits for industry, and are in the course of implementation under the business as usual scenario. However, implementation of business as usual is an inadequate contribution from the sector. In addition, it is also recognised that SMEs can contribute substantial savings as the levels of energy inefficiencies are higher in this sector, and particular regard will be had in the development of the IEC programmes to the requirements of SMEs in the industrial sector.

The IEC will prepare and disseminate best practice guidelines, together with individual energy performance indicators, for each process in this sector and the commercial and services sectors. Based on this work, the Minister for Enterprise, Trade and Employment, and industry, will put in place agreements to achieve agreed global energy efficiency benchmarks in all sectors.

The first of the agreements will be put in place within two years as part of a rolling programme, to be fully implemented as soon as possible after 2005. They will, inter alia: -

▶ specify clear targets to be achieved in each sector, and a timetable for achievement;

▶ identify major emitters, and targeted sectors;

▶ provide for an open and transparent system of reporting and monitoring;

▶ outline proposed future action to deal with "free riders" within the sector, if necessary; and

▶ where appropriate, provision will be made for reduced greenhouse gas taxation where the agreements achieve or exceed best industry standards.

Development and Expansion of IEC Programmes

IEC programmes will be developed and expanded to support the achievement of energy efficiency improvements. In addition to the issues identified in the *Green Paper on Sustainable Energy*, a number of key factors will be addressed: -

▶ development of the scope of existing programmes to provide a framework for the implementation of negotiated agreements, including the specification of benchmarks and standards for these agreements;

▶ while the fundamental rationale of negotiated agreements is to give industry, as key beneficiaries of efficiency improvements, the flexibility and responsibility to drive efficiency within their own sector, a proportion of technologies and/or efficiency improvement choices will need increased support or a prioritisation of support to increase their penetration rates. Current support programmes will be examined and refocused to target these;

▶ identification of appropriate measures such as an information/education campaign to address perceptions concerning scope for efficiency improvements within the sector, and to provide information and advice on best practice; and

▶ exploitation of the potential for businesses and market forces to improve market penetration of more efficient products and in marketing energy efficiency advice.

Industry will also be expected to maximise the market penetration of more efficient products and to enlarge consumers' choice of energy efficient appliances, etc. Ireland is a technology taker in respect of most domestic and other appliances, and accordingly has the scope to ensure a preference for the most energy efficient products. This will be achieved through a negotiated agreement between the Minister for Enterprise, Trade and Employment and the distributive and retail sectors.

Energy Efficiency Improvements – Additional Measures

Supporting measures will include: -

▶ development of an "early warning" monitoring and review mechanism to assess progress and assist in the exchange of advice and information on best practice, with particular regard to monitoring the implementation of negotiated agreements;

▶ the EPA will develop guidelines for reporting systems for emission levels and reductions achieved at company level, compatible with international reporting requirements, and will monitor emissions from IPPC licensed operators;

▶ identification and support of necessary research on new technologies and the application of new technological improvements; and

▶ expanded consumer based programmes to influence consumer behaviour.

Fuel Switching

Where feasible, the option of fuel switching will be pursued in the sequence: - electricity[15] ➡ coal ➡ heavy fuel oils ➡ light oils ➡ gas oil ➡ gas ➡ green electricity. Maximum conversion of industrial use of fuels towards the least greenhouse gas intensive will be encouraged, inter alia, through the market mechanisms of emissions trading and greenhouse gas taxation. Particular regard will be had to distinguish between high-carbon energy sources used in areas not critical for competitiveness (e.g. space heating) and fuels used for process purposes, to allow for higher taxation on non-critical uses of energy.

The IEC will also target the efficient use of the most appropriate fuel from an emissions perspective. In the case of fuel switching to electricity, this will only be appropriate where increasing end-use efficiencies through the use of more efficient electro-technologies can be achieved. The expansion of the use of CHP, where environmentally and economically efficient, will be an important element in achieving greenhouse gas efficiencies in the sector.

---

[15] Location of electricity at the top of the fuel switching ladder occurs when comparison is based on carbon content of generation, where account is taken of transmission losses, and where used for inefficient purposes such as space heating.

Process Substitution

Process emissions from the **cement sector** are a significant contribution to overall Irish greenhouse gas emissions, as almost all cement produced in Ireland is from limestone, although Pulverised Fly Ash (PFA), a by-product of power generation, is also used. Ceasing of coal firing at Moneypoint would reduce domestic sources for PFA. However, alternative sources are available abroad, including Ground Granulated Blast Furnace Slag (GGBFS), a by-product of primary steel production. When careful attention is paid to quality of supply and manufacture, this can act as an acceptable substitute for and/or additive to cement for a large range of applications. The manufacture of cement from GGBFS generates a small fraction of the greenhouse gas emissions from standard limestone based Portland Cement, as there are no process emissions in the conversion to cement, and no energy input for heating is required.

A negotiated agreement will be made by the Departments of Enterprise, Trade and Employment and Environment and Local Government with the industry to ensure that the reductions in emissions achieved are at the global benchmark for industry best practice. Additional environmental and economic benefits will arise, with the introduction of a price-competitive alternative to cement produced from traditional sources.

Process emissions (in addition to emissions from the consumption of gas for energy purposes) are also generated in the conversion of natural gas to ammonia in the manufacture of nitrogenous **fertiliser**. Measures to reduce the use of chemical fertilisers in agriculture (see Chapter 8) will enable a reduction in the amount of product manufactured, and the resulting emissions. A negotiated agreement between the sector and the Departments of Enterprise, Trade and Employment and Agriculture, Food and Rural Development will be put in place to ensure that further reductions in emissions at the global benchmark for industry best practice are achieved.

Industrial Gases

These are the most potent greenhouse gases. Their use will increase due to their replacement of ozone depleting substances, (particularly important in the pharmaceutical sector) and the lack of alternatives in some applications. However, where there are suitable alternatives, the use of these gases will be reduced to a minimum, and if possible, eliminated.

In the implementation of relevant measures, particular regard will be had to the progress of measures to reduce and/or replace these gases in similar companies in the relevant sectors at the global level. Companies will be required to benchmark themselves to the best worldwide efforts to replace or reduce emissions, and support will be given, through the Research, Technological Development and Innovation element of the Productive Sector Operational Programme to make Ireland a centre of excellence for the substitution of these gases.

Because of the anticipated increase in the use of these gases in the economy, their potency (GWPs hundreds to thousands of times higher than CO_2) and their entirely human origin (with alternatives as an option in most applications), it is intended to discourage any new uses in the economy: - in this regard, the examination of inward and indigenous investment proposals and opportunities from the perspective of impact on greenhouse gas emissions will have particular relevance to these gases.

PFCs

Emissions savings from the semi-conductor industry will be achieved through a range of actions including: -

▸ replacement with more benign substitutes;

▸ reduction of the amount used, if replacement is not possible; and

▸ capture and reuse; disposal/destruction if reuse is not feasible.

Reductions will be achieved through a variety of means: -

▸ in addition to the current agreements between the member companies of the European Electronic Component Manufacturers Association, the Minister for Enterprise, Trade and Employment will negotiate an agreement with this sector to be put in place within 2 years, to reduce emissions of industrial gases. These agreements will include commitments to investing in the necessary research and development to identify and bring into use non-emitting technologies;

▸ the IPPC process will continue to be used to secure the reduction of emissions using BAT;

▸ emission charges, including taxation, encouraging the full range of reduction options;

▸ where feasible, and subject to developments at international level, these gases will be included in emissions trading arrangements; and

▸ labelling, training and certification, technical standards.

HFCs

The main uses of HFCs are as commercial replacements for ozone-depleting CFCs and HCFCs being phased out under the Montreal Protocol. The key areas of application include: -

refrigerants, including stationary and mobile (automotive) air-conditioning units; production of rigid foam (foam-blowing); aerosols; solvents; sterilising agents; fire-extinguishing agents.

A number of approaches are available for reducing emissions of HFCs: -

▸ "no use", if HFCs are not essential i.e. restricting HFC use to essential uses when no alternatives exist; this will apply in particular to the refrigeration sector where alternative technologies to HFC use exist, or are in rapid development. In the event that alternative technologies require the use of additional energy in operation, measures will have regard to overall life-cycle analysis on a greenhouse gas emissions basis, and where HFC use is preferred, stringent controls on amounts used, leakage rates and provision for recovery will be incorporated;

▸ avoidance of HFCs having relatively high GWP;

▸ avoidance of non-closed systems, i.e. relatively "leaky", applications, including automotive air-conditioning;

▸ maximising emission control through improved housekeeping practices and recycling;

▸ identification and use of non-HFC agents in foam blowing (elimination of use by 2008 is feasible and will be the target for the negotiated agreement between the industry and the Department of Enterprise, Trade and Employment); and

▸ in the case of fire-fighting equipment a negotiated agreement between the Department of the Environment and Local Government and the industry requiring a rigorous analysis of use in each case will be developed, with an objective of eliminating its use in line with legal requirements and best practice in other countries.

The measures identified for PFCs will be applied to HFCs also. Negotiated agreements relating to this family of gases will incorporate requirements on improved emission monitoring, measures to reduce leakage (including leakage reduction targets and codes of practice), life-cycle management and recycling, efficiency improvements to refrigeration equipment and replacement by alternatives.

Additional measures to be taken will include: -

▸ disincentives, including a regulatory approach and/or additional taxation, for the purchase of cars with air conditioning using HFCs, allied to the development of best practice guides for use and servicing, to minimise leakages; and

▸ taxation of products emitting, or whose production requires the emission, of HFCs.

SF_6

This is the gas with the highest GWP, viz it is 23,900 times more potent than CO_2. The main uses of SF_6 are electrical insulation in power transmission equipment – over 80% of SF_6 is used in high voltage electrical switching gear and circuit breakers, and some specific applications in electronics. Equipment using SF_6 is built to a high international standard and emissions are therefore quite low.

The emissions controls which will be put in place for SF_6 are similar to those used for PFCs and HFCs.

TARGETS FOR THE INDUSTRY, COMMERCIAL AND SERVICES SECTOR

Industry

Large-scale industry is generally modern and has in the relatively recent past adopted many available technologies for improving energy efficiencies. Typical investment cycles are likely to mean that the next optimum time for investing in significant efficiencies will be close to or during the commitment period, although environmental licensing, the advent of CHP and other technologies, and the introduction of economic instruments are likely to accelerate the investment opportunities. Accordingly, the efficiency improvements proposed in this Strategy are small individually, and occur in a diverse range of firms, including many SMEs, at a range of prices per tonne of CO_2 equivalent reduction achieved. Significant reductions below business as usual can be achieved through the adoption of available energy efficiencies, with up to 1 Mt CO_2 reductions achievable at low cost. In excess of another 1 Mt CO_2 reductions could be achieved at a range of costs up to £200 per tonne.

Targets	
"No regrets"/low cost energy efficiency gains	0.75 Mt CO_2
Up to £75 tonne CO_2 efficiency measures	0.25 Mt CO_2
Process Substitution for Cement	0.5 Mt CO_2
Industrial Gases	0.5 Mt CO_2 equivalent
TOTAL	**2.0 Mt CO_2 equivalent per annum**

Commercial and Services

Energy efficiency measures can be expected to reduce emissions below business as usual by **0.175 Mt CO$_2$** at low or no cost (assuming 50% uptake of "no regret"/low cost measures). It is difficult to disaggregate some reductions between this sector and the Built Environment and Residential Sector (Chapter 6), because of the continuum across sectors (e.g. building standards, efficiency improvements).

Chapter 8
Agriculture

EMISSIONS/PROJECTIONS FOR AGRICULTURE SECTOR

The agricultural sector represents 5.2% of GDP, 8.7% of employment and 7.2% of exports[16]. Three quarters of the land area of Ireland is used for agriculture and forestry, and over 80% of the area under agriculture is devoted to grass, with beef and milk production currently accounting for 68% of gross agricultural output.

Agricultural emissions of greenhouse gases are very significant in the Irish context. Greenhouse gas emissions in 1990 from the agricultural sector were 34.6% of total national emissions, the highest of all sectors. Agriculture was responsible for 84.1% of CH_4 emissions in 1990, expected to rise to 90.1% by 2010 and 78.7% of N_2O emissions in 1990 (expected to be 77.4% in 2010). The high GWP of these gases, at 21 times and 310 times that of CO_2 respectively, means that their weight within the overall basket of gases increases accordingly. For most developed countries, with a higher proportion of economic wealth arising from heavy industry and less from agriculture, CO_2 represents approximately 80% of the basket of gases. For Ireland, with a comparatively greater proportion of economic production from agriculture, CO_2 represented 58.7% of the national basket in 1990, with CH_4 and N_2O representing 40.8%.

Business as usual projections predict that agricultural emissions will increase during the period 1990 to 2010 by 3.3% in aggregate. Ruminant emissions (enteric fermentation), manure management and emissions from soils will increase by 0.2%, 6.3% and 5.1% respectively. Given the projections of significant increases in CO_2 and industrial gases in this period, the overall agriculture contribution is expected to fall to 25.6% of the basket of emissions by 2010.

The main sources of agricultural emissions are enteric fermentation (ruminant digestion), responsible for 51.1% of total emissions from agriculture, and agricultural soils and manures which are responsible for 34.6% and 10.4% respectively of emissions from the sector (1990 data). Cattle are the dominant source of CH_4 from ruminant digestion, and while emissions are directly linked to the size of the national herd, opportunities also exist to reduce the levels of emissions per animal. The quantity of nitrogenous fertiliser spread, and the breakdown of this in the soil, are the main determinants of the amount of N_2O emitted from agriculture.

MEASURES TO CONTROL GREENHOUSE GAS EMISSIONS

A critical challenge for this Strategy is to balance the environmental objective of greenhouse gas emissions reductions with the economic and social objective of protecting farm income and maintaining the highest possible number of farm households.

Policy Reform at EU level

Policy formulation at EU level, in the context of the post-Agenda 2000 arrangements in particular, will afford an opportunity to consider matters of financial support for agreed common and coordinated policies and measures to address greenhouse gas emissions. Ireland will support appropriate proposals at EU level seeking necessary adjustments to CAP mechanisms to pursue climate change abatement action through further integration of environmental considerations into agriculture policy. In this regard, it will be emphasised that reductions in greenhouse gas emissions from the agriculture sector are more important for Ireland than for other Member States in meeting national targets.

| GRAPH 6 | BREAKDOWN OF GREENHOUSE GAS EMISSIONS FROM AGRICULTURE (fossil fuel combustion (CO_2 Agriculture) ruminants (Enteric Fermentation), manures, and soils (Agricultural Soils) FOR 1990, 1998 AND 2010 PROJECTIONS |

Graph data (kt):

	1990	1998	2010
CO_2 Agriculture	719	807	869
Enteric Fermentation	9,506	10,365	9,523
Manure Management	1,938	2,208	2,061
Agricultural Soils	6,446	7,125	6,774
Total Agriculture	18,608	20,505	19,227

[16] 12.7% of GDP, 11.8% of employment and 12% of exports if agri-food sector is included - this covers agriculture, food, drinks and tobacco.

Reduction of Methane (CH$_4$) from National Herd

Reflecting the central position of cattle production enterprises in Irish agriculture, CH$_4$ emissions from ruminant animals constitute roughly one fifth of Ireland's total emissions of greenhouse gases, greater than greenhouse gas emissions from power generation. Reductions in this area could have a significant impact on Ireland's total emissions.

The main contributors of CH$_4$ from ruminant animals (1990) are cattle (86.8%) and sheep (12.6%), with 80.0% of emissions from cattle coming from non-dairy herds. Total cattle numbers have risen significantly between 1990 and 1999 (15.2%), within which the suckler herd increased by 66.4%. Business as usual projections are for numbers to decline from the 1999 level by 2010 (5% drop for total cattle numbers) but total numbers will be still above 1990 levels (+9.6%).

The **objective** will be to secure CH$_4$ reductions of 1.2 Mt CO$_2$ equivalent in emissions from livestock. These will be achieved by reducing stock numbers below business as usual expectations for 2010, on the basis that the required CH$_4$ reduction is equivalent to a reduction of 10% in livestock numbers over the period. An appropriate balance will be maintained between direct reductions in stock numbers to be achieved based on current EU policies and coupled with extensification and other management measures in REPS, and intensification of the range of the measures identified for the agriculture sector as well as any further appropriate measures applied following dedicated research, and demonstrating equivalent greenhouse gas emissions reductions. Such measures will be applied on a least cost basis to contribute towards meeting the overall 1.2 Mt CO$_2$ equivalent target. Progress will be subject to a two yearly review.

In the development of the programme of reductions of CH$_4$ from livestock, a number of criteria will be met, including: -

▶ maintenance of the maximum number of family farms and meeting the requirements of small and low-income farm families;

▶ identification of viable alternative enterprises to supplement farm income and alternative employment opportunities within the rural environment; and

▶ measures to improve the sustainability of agricultural systems, including the promotion of organic farming (including the necessary supports for training, marketing, processing and distribution).

Government policy for the development of agriculture, food and rural development is set out in a range of policy statements and programmes which include the *National Development Plan 2000 – 2006; Ensuring the Future – A Strategy for Rural Development in Ireland – a white paper on Rural Development;* the *Programme for Prosperity and Fairness;* and the *Agri-Food 2010 Plan of Action.* The action taken to deliver the targets proposed in the Strategy will build on existing policy requirements and the need for consultation as appropriate including with the farming social partners. The arrangements flowing from the Agenda 2000 Agreement provide the basis for the principal supports for agriculture over the coming years. Negotiations for the post-Agenda 2000 period are expected to commence by 2006, and should provide an opportunity to consider further responses to climate change.

The measures and programmes outlined above will be developed by the Department of Agriculture, Food and Rural Development in partnership with the agriculture sector in the context of the overall need to coordinate measures through the Inter-Departmental Climate Change Team.

For each one percentage point change in overall 2010 stock numbers in the cattle herd, emissions increase or decrease by 0.12 Mt CO$_2$ equivalent. The direct costs of reductions at farm level are estimated at £90 – £95 per tonne CO$_2$ equivalent (1999 prices), and direct costs including upstream and downstream industries are estimated to be of the order of £150 per tonne CO$_2$ equivalent. These costs do not, however, include synergies with other policy priorities (e.g. the capacity to convert additional land to forestry production), nor the economic return at farm level from other alternative land uses for the land freed from cattle production. Furthermore, as reductions will be achieved through the adaptation of existing agriculture schemes (e.g. REPS), further CAP reform and a reduction of land available for agriculture through the expansion of the forestry programme, net costs of measures to reduce CH$_4$ emissions specifically will be considerably below this.

Reduction in Emissions per Animal

A research programme will be undertaken by Teagasc to identify feeding regimes, appropriate to Irish conditions, that reduce CH$_4$ emissions from individual animals. The objective will be to reduce the level of emissions per animal, while maintaining productivity levels. While in some respects the technologies to achieve significant reductions are at an early stage of development, there are good grounds for targeting up to 0.5 Mt CO$_2$ equivalent of the overall greenhouse gas reduction from the national herd on the basis of appropriate research projects on technologies to reduce emission factors being funded and facilitated as a priority. It is recognised that the full achievement of this element of the CH$_4$

reduction will not be available in respect of the full commitment period, and the full target is to be achieved by 2012. The following list of measures with potential to reduce emissions per animal will be prioritised in research: -

- use of feed additives;
- probiotics and engineering;
- changes in level of concentrate feeding;
- changes in the system of cattle production with a focus on finishing at a younger age; and
- improved feeding and management at farm level.

CH_4 emissions reductions per animal would also be significantly facilitated by adjustments to CAP support measures to encourage lower stocking intensity levels by reaching slaughter age earlier; Ireland will seek these adjustments in the medium term.

The ongoing review of this Strategy will incorporate appropriate measures identified by the research where the reductions potential is quantified and the measures involved are subsequently applied.

Fertiliser Use

Total nitrogen applied to soils has increased by 7.2% between 1990 and 1999, and on a business as usual basis, is expected to further increase by 2010 to 10.7% above 1990 levels. Current livestock grazing systems are very inefficient in the use of both chemical and organic nitrogen. Significant quantities are lost to the atmosphere as nitrous oxide (N_2O) (and also ammonia (NH_3), a contributor to local and transboundary air pollution). There are losses also to surface waters and groundwaters, contributing to water pollution. These, and the consequential environmental damage, are unsustainable.

N_2O emissions arising from nitrogenous fertiliser spreading will be reduced by 10% below the business as usual levels expected for 2010, with a consequential emissions reduction of 0.9 Mt of CO_2 equivalent. This reduction in N_2O emissions, based on reduced fertiliser use, will be supplemented by a number of measures, including:-

- adjustments to the requirements of support schemes. Under the CAP Rural Development Plan 2000 – 2006, farmers participating in the agriculture measures covered by the Plan other than REPS (Compensatory Allowances and Early Retirement), and in a number of other Schemes including On-Farm Investment and Farm Waste Management, will be required to follow Good Farming Practice which is defined in the Plan. This will include a requirement to conform with Teagasc recommendations on nutrient management (including proper use of nitrogen and chemical and organic

fertilisers), and to comply with the 1996 Code of Good Agricultural Practice to Protect Waters from Pollution by Nitrates. Farmers participating in REPS itself will be required to follow a farm nutrient management plan to REPS specifications (which are higher than those in the Code) for the total area of the farm;

- use of slow release inhibitors;
- efficient recycling of slurry and dirty water;
- the use of slurries and manures in weather and ground conditions which maximise the uptake of nitrogen by the soil and plant growth (including restrictions in the application of chemical nitrogen and animal waste applications in the September to January period);
- growing of more forage maize and incorporation of slurry into the soil (ploughing in farmyard manure and slurry); and
- bandspreading of animal waste.

The full impact of these measures remains to be quantified by appropriate research and application. Combining the reduction of 10% fertiliser use with the additional measures identified, N_2O emissions could be reduced by up to 0.9 Mt CO_2 equivalent below the business as usual projections by 2010.

The option of utilising taxation on artificial fertilisers will be kept under review in light of the success of the management measures set out above.

Strengthen Relationship with Forestry Policy

A change in land use arising from the conversion of agricultural land from animal production to forestry ensures a double dividend: - a reduction of CH_4 and N_2O emissions and additional sequestration of carbon from the atmosphere. To the extent that this evolution of agriculture policy is driven by climate change considerations, enhanced sequestration of carbon will be a valuable part of the response of the agriculture sector.

The administration of **REPS** now places greater emphasis on forestry as an option. The Rural Development Plan 2000 – 2006, covering both REPS and Forestry, includes a proposal for the integration of the two measures to ensure coherence and to maximise environmental benefits including carbon sequestration. For all applications, it is proposed that the assessment at farm level by REPS planners will include identification of land suitable for productive afforestation. Any such areas will be notified to the Forest Service. The necessary training and guidance will be given to REPS planners on the criteria to be applied on prioritisation of land use between forestry and agriculture. Such criteria will include landscape, biodiversity, pollution control, carbon sequestration, wildlife and productivity/suitability of land for forestry and agriculture.

The Departments of Agriculture, Food and Rural Development and Marine and Natural Resources will continue to review and adjust, as necessary, the conditions for payment of REPS premia, and restructure premia in respect of afforestation, to underpin the attractiveness of suitable forestry development and avoid negative competition between agriculture and forestry. In the context of a mid-term review of REPS in three years' time, the Departments will review the possibility of encouraging more afforestation on the projected 70,000 farms participating in the Scheme.

The current estimate is that on average these 70,000 farmers will afforest about one hectare of land each by 2010 as part of a planned afforestation programme. The carbon sequestration to be achieved specifically within the agriculture sector, in addition to the sequestration to be achieved within the national forestry programme (see Chapter 9), is predicted to be 0.25 Mt CO_2 equivalent. Due to the necessity to adopt a conservative approach to the calculation of afforestation as a Kyoto sink pending finalisation of the international negotiations at COP6, the calculation of this target will be reviewed by the Inter-Departmental Climate Change Team in 2001.

Extensification and Set-Aside

The potential for developing short-rotation biomass for energy generation as an alternative land use where animal numbers are reduced, and for set-aside land, will be developed in conjunction with the renewable energy programme. Biomass is carbon-neutral in the energy cycle, and it will be developed in a manner that reduces greenhouse gas emissions overall. Life-cycle analysis will be undertaken in each case to ensure that any emissions arising from the farming practices employed (soil disturbance, fertiliser use, harvesting and transport) are less than would have occurred from conventional land uses and energy sources.

Animal Waste

Animal wastes have been identified by the European Commission as technologically the most promising area for reducing CH_4 emissions in the agriculture sector, although the proportion of agricultural emissions from this source is relatively small. The use of anaerobic digesters with energy recovery will be integrated with measures to promote renewable energy, on an individual enterprise basis where appropriate through IPC licensing, or where greater quantities are required, on a community or other combined basis (e.g. in association with the treatment of municipal waste). There is significant potential for synergies with other policy priorities, (e.g. improved nutrient management, reduced odour problems, support for rural development and displacement of fossil fuels from electricity production). However, there are a number of technical and financial barriers to the extensive use of anaerobic digesters, and in the implementation of the Strategy, these will be explored by the relevant Government Departments with interests in promoting bioenergy production in order to remove any unnecessary obstacles to the deployment of the technology at farm and community level.

Best Practice Guidelines

The 1996 *Code of Good Agricultural Practice for the Protection of Waters from Pollution from Nitrates,* while introduced with the aim of reducing water pollution, includes recommendations on best practice in the use of chemical nitrogenous fertilisers which would if followed have the effect of reducing N_2O emissions. Participants in the agriculture measures under the CAP Rural Development Plan 2000 – 2006 (except REPS which has specific standards) will be required to meet specified standards of *Good Farming Practice* reflecting legislative and other requirements in a number of areas including nutrient management. These standards will be kept under review during the period of the Plan and will be amended as necessary to reflect legislative changes and other relevant developments, including climate change requirements.

IPC Licensing

Intensive agriculture is subject to IPC licensing; the requirement to use Best Available Techniques (BAT) under the EU IPPC Directive will ensure that all appropriate preventive measures, including CH_4 and energy recovery from manures, are fully taken in enterprises subject to these controls.

International Emissions Trading

The potential modalities for trading of emissions from the agriculture sector will be kept under review and pursued by Ireland in the context of the finalisation of the arrangements for international emissions trading. The Government recognises that this instrument may provide an additional mechanism to deliver on the reduction targets set for the agriculture sector.

TARGETS FOR THE AGRICULTURE SECTOR

Reduction of CH_4 from national herd	
Objective	1.2 Mt CO_2 equivalent
of which Feeding Regimes	0.5 Mt CO_2 equivalent, in a longer term perspective (by 2012 and beyond) depending on outcome of research programme, and at some cost savings, as many lower emission feeding regimes are profitable in their own right
Fertiliser Use	0.9 Mt CO_2 equivalent
On-Farm Forestry Sequestration	0.25 Mt CO_2 equivalent
Manure Management	0.06 Mt CO_2 equivalent
TOTAL	**2.41 Mt CO_2 equivalent per annum**

While **costs** could be of the order of **£100m p.a.**, the total cost to the sector will depend on the balance of measures implemented to reflect the overall limitation commitment for the sector and may be offset by increased income from alternative land uses. The actions for the sector meet other policy objectives and costs will be assigned proportionately.

Chapter 9
Sinks

EMISSIONS/PROJECTIONS FOR SINKS

Approximately 9% of Ireland's land area, the smallest proportion in the EU, is covered by forest. The afforestation programme outlined in *Growing for the Future, A Strategic Plan for the Development of the Forestry Sector in Ireland* sets national planting targets of 20,000ha per annum from 2001 to 2030, doubling forest land cover to 17%. Due to various constraints only around half the planting programme (planned at 25,000ha per annum to 2000) has been achieved in the past number of years.

Irish climatic and soil conditions are very suitable for rapid tree growth, notably for certain species of conifer, and the rate of timber production is significantly higher than elsewhere in Europe and on a par with the most favourable conditions in the world. Sitka spruce has one of the highest growth rates of any tree species in Europe and is a highly efficient storer of carbon. It is recognised that from the biodiversity perspective, forest policy should favour broadleaves to the greatest extent possible, and that the current 20% target for planting of broadleaves is inadequate. The reduction of Sitka spruce planting to 60%, as outlined in the *Strategic Plan,* represents the sector's commitment to achieving increased biodiversity, albeit at some cost to forest production. Just over half the national forest stock is owned by Coillte Teoranta, the State forestry company. Significant support is now being given to planting by the private sector, and planting by the private sector now exceeds that by Coillte.

Under the Kyoto Protocol, carbon sequestration by the forestry stock arising from afforestation, deforestation and reforestation activities since 1990, i.e. the planting/deforestation programme since this date may be counted towards meeting Ireland's net greenhouse gas growth limitation target.

Methodologies for accounting for forestry sequestration under the Kyoto Protocol have not yet been agreed. As a number of significant questions regarding the methodologies for incorporating sinks into the Kyoto Protocol process have been raised in the *Special Report on Land Use, Land Use Change and Forestry* by the IPCC[17], published in June 2000, a conservative approach has been taken to calculating total sequestration rates for the purpose of the sector's overall contribution to the Kyoto commitment. However, by 2010, it is estimated that for the likely methodologies, the sequestration rate of forestry (above-ground woody mass only) planted under the *Growing for the Future*

Strategy will be 2.1 Mt CO_2 equivalent per annum by 2010, assuming full achievement of the target. If only half the programme is implemented, the sequestration rate will be 2/3 rds this, at 1.4 Mt CO_2 equivalent[18].

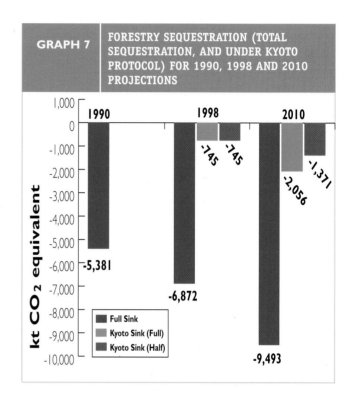

| GRAPH 7 | FORESTRY SEQUESTRATION (TOTAL SEQUESTRATION, AND UNDER KYOTO PROTOCOL) FOR 1990, 1998 AND 2010 PROJECTIONS |

---

[17] Summary for Policymakers is available at http://www.ipcc.ch/pub/reports.htm
[18] For the purpose of counting the national forestry sink, a further reduction of 50% to is conservatively assumed take account *inter alia* of the low rate of sequestration while forestry stocks are under 20 years of age.

ENHANCING GREENHOUSE GAS SEQUESTRATION

Review Forest Strategy

The overall aim of *Growing for the Future is* "to develop forestry to a scale and in a manner which maximises its contribution to national economic and social well-being on a sustainable basis and which is compatible with the protection of the environment". However, *Growing for the Future* was prepared prior to the Kyoto Protocol, and it will now be reassessed to ensure that the issues associated with carbon sequestration, and in particular timing, are fully taken into account in its implementation. The forestry planting rate must be maximised as early as possible prior to the commencement of the commitment period, as growth rates, and hence sequestration, are fastest in the middle years of the forestry cycle. The implications for rural development and the sustainability of rural communities will also be taken into account in the review and implementation of *Growing for the Future.*

In assessing the relative economic benefits of the forestry programme and REPS and other agriculture support schemes which impinge on the programme, the economic benefits of enhanced carbon sequestration will be taken into account. Account will also be taken of the relative benefits of forestry planting on different soil types: - e.g. planting on poor quality mineral soils is preferable, from an overall carbon uptake perspective, to planting on peat soils, and these soils are also least suitable for modern agricultural practices.

The recently commissioned state-of-the-art Geographic Information System (GIS) will help to identify areas suitable for forestry while highlighting potentially contentious afforestation sites, in areas such as riparian zones, National Heritage Areas (NHAs), Special Areas of Conservation (SACs) and Special Protection Areas (SPAs). This will ensure that all future forestry developments will be analysed for compatibility with the requirements of sustainable forestry practice.

The *Irish National Forestry Standard* and the *Code of Best Forest Practice* issued by the Forest Service of the Department of the Marine and Natural Resources establish the framework for adherence to the principles of Sustainable Forest Management (SFM). They provide a mechanism for the complementary assessment of the implications of climate change and other environmental constraints on forestry. The Forest Service has also issued a suite of *Environmental Guidelines* describing, for forest owners, managers and their staff, the range of measures necessary to conform to best practice in forestry management and implementation of SFM.

Virtually 100% of afforestation in Ireland is grant-aided and all grant recipients must conform to the *Environmental Guidelines*. Adherence to these Guidelines by forestry developers is mandatory, with the Forest Service Inspectorate ensuring compliance. All grant-aided plantations are inspected to ensure that they achieve full stocking and the production levels (and thus carbon sequestration levels) assumed in growth and yield models. Furthermore the Forest Inventory and Planning System (FIPS) ensures that the current annual volume increment and standing wood volume are continuously updated.

The scope for **intensification of the afforestation programme** for the Kyoto and successive commitment periods will also be assessed, in view of the ongoing importance of enhancing sinks capacity towards reducing overall greenhouse gas concentrations in the atmosphere and assisting in meeting longer term greenhouse gas reduction requirements.

The above reassessment will also examine the options for planting a higher proportion of faster growing and/or shorter rotation forestry crops e.g. poplars, willows and some other species which have a greater uptake rate over a shorter period. Short rotation forestry is being examined on a pilot basis, and it is recognised that additional levels of integration are required for success, involving cooperation between different interests. Care will also be required to ensure that the equilibrium storage of carbon over several rotations is as great as that arising from the current planting mixture in the forestry programme.

Research and Development

Extensive forest R&D is carried out with an overall objective to increase quality and productivity from all species – and to ensure cost effective and sustainable practices. An important feature of current research programmes is the identification of appropriate native sources of broadleaf planting stock, as the bulk of the expanded broadleaf planting programme is based on imported stock which may not be best suited to Irish conditions. The inclusion of additional criteria, such as meeting biodiversity obligations, reduces somewhat the potential that would be available to sequester carbon if high-yield conifers only were planted. However, conservation of biological diversity may be one of the most effective, practical responses to climate change; conservation of this biological diversity at all levels (e.g. from genes within species to the array of habitat types across the landscape) will permit natural species to adapt as their environment changes.

The research programme will be expanded to contain an element seeking to identify those stocks (and species) which are best suited to maximising the sequestration potential of Irish forests. Further research will also be carried out into the appropriate management techniques, and their dissemination through the forestry sector, to ensure that the additional complexities of the broadleaf sector are provided for and sequestration rates enhanced.

The *National Biodiversity Plan,* in preparation, will also address the requirements of integrating environmental concerns into forestry policy planning.

Additional Categories of Sinks

The Protocol makes provision for the inclusion of additional sinks related to human activities in the agricultural soils and land use change and forestry categories, once the rules, modalities and guidelines for these are agreed at a future Conference of the Parties to the Protocol. These categories must be included in meeting commitments in future commitment periods, and there is an option to include them for the period 2008 – 2012. Analysis of the options and implications for the achievement of the Kyoto Protocol emissions reduction objective in respect of these additional categories have been addressed in the *Special Report on Land Use, Land Use Change and Forestry* by the IPCC.

The relevance of agricultural practices to carbon flows in soils may increase when the methodologies to account for the additional categories are finalised. The Departments of the Marine and Natural Resources, and Agriculture, Food and Rural Development will participate in UN negotiations on this issue, with assistance, as appropriate, from Teagasc, COFORD (the National Council for Forest Research and Development) and 3rd level research institutes. In light of the outcome of the negotiations on additional categories of sinks for the second commitment period, the options for including them in respect of the first commitment period will be addressed at the earliest appropriate time in the context of the ongoing implementation and review of the Strategy.

Inventory Research and Development

Current inventories and projections are only developed for the above-ground portion of the forest stock. Significant amounts of carbon can also be sequestered by root systems and forest litter (possibly 50% more than in woody biomass) but there can be carbon losses from forest soils, especially for forestry planted on peat soils. The recent development of FIPS, which incorporates information on forest soils, is an important resource in determining the full extent of carbon sequestration by the national forest stock. The Department of the Marine and Natural Resources and COFORD, in conjunction with the EPA, will undertake the necessary research to address the shortcomings in the methodologies for inventories and projections, having regard to the developing negotiations on Land Use, Land Use Change and Forestry under the Kyoto Protocol.

TARGET FOR FORESTRY SINKS

This will be very dependent on the outcome of the negotiations on accounting for Kyoto forestry. Assuming the same methodologies as used in determining the EU burden sharing, the **target** (based on full achievement of the forestry programme instead of the c. 50% planting rate over the last few years) would be an additional **0.76 Mt CO_2 equivalent sequestered** in excess of business as usual. Because a conservative approach to the calculations has been adopted pending further progress in the international negotiations at COP6, the calculation of this target will be reviewed by the Inter-Departmental Climate Change Team in 2001.

The **marginal costs** attributable to climate change policy are assumed to be **nil**, as provision is made in the forestry programme for the full programme.

While the forestry sector is an economic actor in its own right, participation in forestry is also an option for other economic sectors, including agriculture and in respect of appropriate land use for cutaway bog at the end of peat removal for electricity or other purposes. In the conversion of land from agriculture (livestock rearing) to forestry there is a double benefit of reduced CH_4 emissions due to the reduction in the national animal herd, a reduction in N_2O emissions due to lower use of nitrogenous fertilisers, and CO_2 uptake through the carbon sequestered in the forestry. In addressing **sectoral equity,** as provided for in Chapter 2, the contribution of these sectors to the forestry programme and the sequestration of carbon in national forest stocks will be taken into account, together with the contribution of the forestry sector itself.

Chapter 10
**Role of Local
Authorities**

NEW FOCUS FOR LOCAL AUTHORITIES

Local Government Reform

Local government is undergoing renewal and reform to meet the needs of the communities it serves more effectively and comprehensively. Strengthened local government will expand its sphere of influence into wider public services and community development. A major Local Government Bill has recently been published and when enacted will modernise and consolidate local government law and provide a sound footing for local authorities to function more effectively. This Bill also provides for greater inclusion of the community in local government and enhances the role of the elected member.

Within the existing framework of local government, decision making structures at political and management levels will be improved through the new Strategic Policy Committee structures. These will enable elected representatives and representatives of sectoral interests to formulate local authority policy in a range of areas including infrastructure and transportation, environmental management and services, housing, social and economic development, energy efficiency and renewable energy. In this regard, new County/City Development Boards led by local government and representative of local decision makers will agree County/City Strategies on Economic, Social and Cultural Development by January 2002.

Local authorities can make an important contribution towards raising awareness and initiating climate change action in local communities. The new structures, within and beyond the traditional framework of local government, will provide an influential, representative local base from which to incorporate climate change abatement considerations into relevant local policies and programmes.

In the development of **performance indicators** to measure the efficiency levels achieved by local authorities, one of the criteria will be the contribution the local authority has made to control and reduce greenhouse gas emissions within their areas of direct responsibility, and towards controls and reductions in their local communities. In addition, energy efficiency targets are set for all public sector organisations, including local authorities, and progress on achievement of these targets will be reported on annually.

Local Energy Agencies (LEAs)

These agencies provide information and advice on energy efficiency and alternative energy at a local level, both for internal local authority functions and also for the wider local community. LEAs make a significant "bottom up" contribution to local authorities' and communities' efforts to reduce emissions from their own activities. Measures have been taken to extend the number of agencies with financial assistance for the first three years from the European Union's SAVE programme. When the EU-funded contracts expire after the first 3 years (for both existing and future agencies), financing will revert to normal block funding arrangements through the Local Government Fund. Agencies have also been asked to pursue local business funding opportunities.

The IEC will support the work of the Agencies with necessary material and technical assistance. LEAs will provide direct assistance to the local authorities including in relation to improving energy efficiency in water, lighting and effluent services, social and private housing, administration buildings, integration of energy planning into the local planning process and the development of renewable energy solutions to problems such as waste management. These measures will, of course, lead to financial savings to local authorities arising from reduced energy consumption. The agencies will also provide independent information, training and technical advice to the wider public on energy efficiency and renewable energy.

One of the conditions for EU assistance to LEAs is the establishment of partnerships with similar agencies and local authorities in other EU and applicant states. The EU SAVE programme also provides ongoing financial support for the exchange of experience in energy efficiency and renewable energy, both through the establishment of networks and through an annual call for proposals for financing of specific projects. These programmes provide local authorities with access to best practice in an EU context.

International Good Practice

Local authorities play a particularly important role in relation to greenhouse gas reductions in a number of sectors, including opportunities in the planning and transport sectors, housing and waste disposal, and in relation to emissions from their own activities. The International Council for Local Environmental Initiatives (ICLEI) has established a global campaign – Cities for Climate Protection (CCP) – to "build a worldwide movement of local governments who adopt policies and implement measures that achieve measurable reductions in local greenhouse gas emissions; improve air quality; and enhance urban liveability and sustainability". The campaign includes more than 175 local authorities around the world, representing 5% of global greenhouse gas emissions: - the target is to recruit local authorities representing 10% of emissions. Local authorities are mobilised to reduce emissions through the identification of sources and quantification of emissions at local level, the setting of reduction targets, and the development and implementation of Local Action Plans, with regular reports on progress.

The CCP campaign also operates a variety of technical assistance projects that focus on innovative financing strategies for energy efficiency measures in local authority buildings, reducing emissions through effective waste management programmes and land use planning, and tackling emissions from the transport sector. Emissions from all these sectors are dealt with in detail elsewhere in this Strategy; the ICLEI initiative provides an important focus for direct action by local authorities complementing the actions of others.

Dublin Corporation has joined the CCP campaign; other local authorities are encouraged to participate actively in the process to learn from international best practice and adapt local government experience elsewhere to Irish circumstances.

Local Agenda 21

This defines and articulates sustainable development considerations at a local/regional level and identifies how they can best be approached and achieved. Consultation and consensus-building are essential elements of Local Agenda 21. Local authorities have important responsibilities to raise awareness and intensify action in support of sustainable development at local level and are developing and implementing Local Agenda 21 initiatives for their areas, which must of necessity have local ownership. The Local Agenda 21 Officers (networked at regional and national levels) provide a forum for exchanging experience and good practice as well as assisting a coherent implementation of Local Agenda 21 across the various local authorities.

LOCAL AUTHORITIES AND SECTORAL RESPONSIBILITIES

The contribution of local authorities to sectoral responses towards the achievement of the national target is dealt with in previous Chapters e.g. in relation to land use planning,

development control, transport, the services sector, housing, energy planning and awareness raising.

Local authorities have particular responsibilities in relation to waste management, the source of 17% of CH_4 emissions in 1990. Accordingly, the potential for greenhouse gas emissions reductions from this source is addressed here.

EMISSIONS/PROJECTIONS FOR WASTE

Emissions from waste contributed 15.6% of CH_4 in 1990, equivalent to 3.9% of the 1990 basket of gases. Achievement of national waste management targets, in particular very substantial diversion of waste away from landfill, should lead to an estimated 80% reduction in CH_4 emissions from landfill by 2015, equivalent to 1.7 Mt CO_2 equivalent.

Emissions of CH_4 from the waste sector arise from the anaerobic decomposition, in landfill, of wastes containing carbon. Up to 50% of this can be recovered from modern landfill in practice, and flared off (converting the CH_4 to CO_2), or used for the production of electricity.

MEASURES TO CONTROL GREENHOUSE GAS EMISSIONS

While the target set for CH_4 reduction is ambitious, it is very necessary to the achievement of Ireland's Kyoto commitment, and desirable for a range of other reasons also.

The marginal cost of achieving a climate change dividend through modernised waste management practice, as set out in *Changing our Ways*, in addition to meeting its primary environmental and other objectives, is minimal. Conversely, lost opportunities for achieving reductions in emissions from the waste sector would require compensatory savings to be identified and obtained elsewhere in the economy, adding to the overall burden for other sectors.

In implementing waste management plans, local authorities will be asked to identify and emphasise the climate change gains, and ensure that these are incorporated into the detailed analysis of management and treatment options. It will be important that sectors, and the public, currently utilising landfill participate to the fullest extent possible in the diversion of waste from landfill. The business community, for example, is contributing to the achievement of Ireland's targets through the diversion of biodegradable waste from landfill by means of individual efforts to facilitate recovery of paper and similar wastes, as well as support for Repak Ltd., which operates a packaging waste recovery scheme aimed at meeting Ireland's targets under relevant EU legislation.

TARGETS FOR WASTE

These are established in *Changing our Ways*, and are to be achieved over a fifteen year timescale. In this regard, the targets for the Kyoto timescale to 2008 – 2012 are established on the basis of maximising early action and early capacity to capture the "no regret" and least cost options.

A reduction of 60% below 1990 levels in CH_4 emissions deriving from the pursuit of policies and provision of new treatment infrastructure in accordance with *Changing our Ways* should be achievable by 2010. Accordingly, the overall emissions from the waste sector in the commitment period are expected to be **0.85 Mt CO_2 equivalent**, or 1.2% of the basket of gases at that time.

The installation of landfill gas recovery in the period to 2010 will double existing landfill gas generating capacity (from 12 MW to 25 MW installed capacity), giving 200,000 MWh additional electricity per annum. Thermal treatment facilities are expected to provide 500,000 MWh electricity and 360,000 MWh utilisable heat per annum. This energy recovery from landfill and thermal treatment will displace **0.8 Mt CO_2 equivalent** from fossil fuel electricity generation.

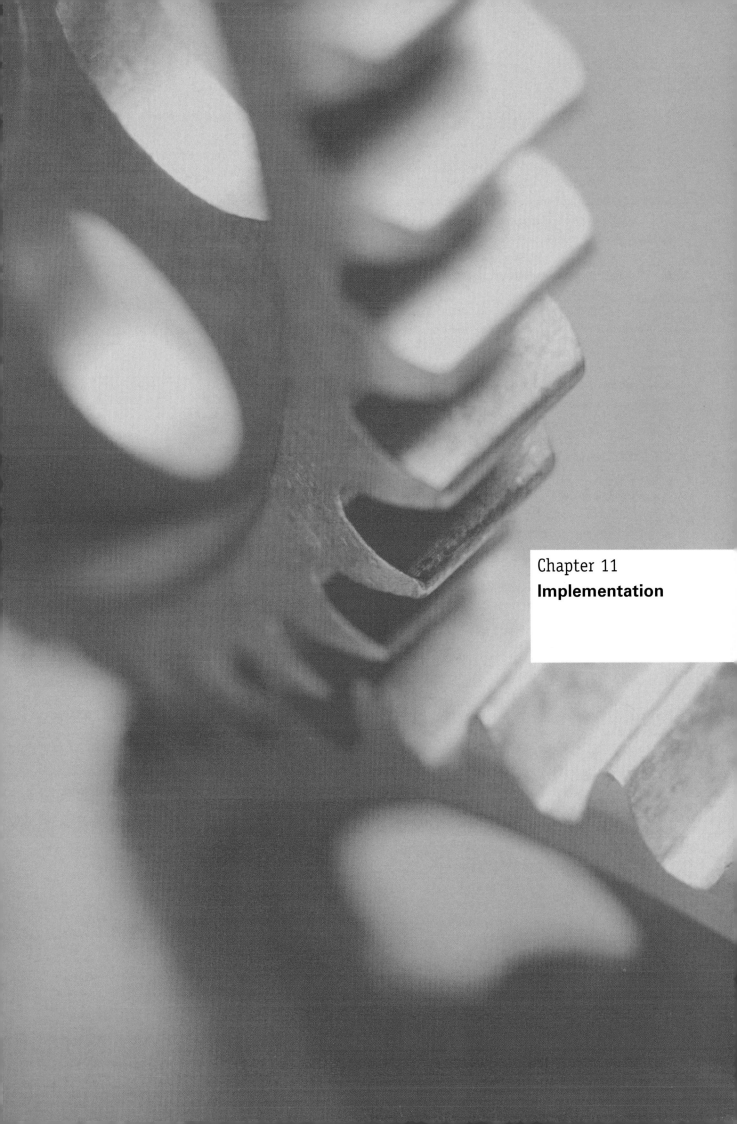

Chapter 11
Implementation

IMPLEMENTATION

The Minister for the Environment and Local Government will ensure that the necessary implementation and monitoring mechanisms are put in place to deliver this Strategy. This will involve a high degree of policy integration across major sectoral areas, and detailed coordination of action at a cross-sectoral level.

From Framework to Action

The Government's commitment to move from Strategy to action is set out in Chapter 1. All relevant Government Departments and Agencies will undertake the necessary analytical and other work to develop and implement the many necessary measures indicated in the Strategy to meet our climate change obligation. Staffing and other resources will be required to realise this step, and will be provided by the relevant Ministers and the Government as necessary.

Climate Change Team

The Government has agreed that a cross-Departmental Climate Change Team will be established at a senior policy level to secure early implementation of measures in this Strategy. This team will be assisted by a cross-Departmental/Agency Support Unit comprising environmental, relevant sectoral and economics expertise to underpin the necessary analysis for implementation of specific measures. The Climate Change Team will establish necessary consultative arrangements with Social Partners, and will report to the Environmental Network of Government Departments on a regular basis. The biennial review of the Strategy will also be undertaken by the Team in consultation with Comhar.

Emissions Trading

In the light of the continuing evolution of negotiations on international emissions trading, the Emissions Trading Advisory Group will be invited to continue providing advice and recommendations to the Minister for the Environment and Local Government on how Ireland should be most appropriately positioned to take part.

Analysis and Assessment of Taxation Measures

This will be overseen by the Tax Strategy Group (TSG) (chaired by the Department of Finance). Preparatory work will be undertaken by the Green Tax Group, a sub-group of the TSG also chaired by the Department of Finance. Necessary supporting analysis will be commissioned prior to preparation of proposals for the Tax Strategy Group. The assessment and analysis work of the Groups will be completed in time for introduction of appropriate initial measures in Budget 2002.

Costs and Benefits of Measures

For each sector, the **costs** of undertaking action are identified in the Strategy in broad terms, together with the reductions in greenhouse gas emissions. This process does not in all cases quantify the economic **benefits** of taking action, either at a national economic level or at a sectoral level (e.g. efficiency improvements that improve the profitability of enterprises, competitiveness and employment opportunities). Gains also arise in synergies with other major policy objectives (e.g. improved security of energy supply through greater use of renewable energy, reduced environmental damage through better controls on the use of nitrogenous fertilisers). Neither do anticipated implementation costs at a sectoral level include the costs of inaction (e.g. the costs of adaptation to climate change, or future costs of non-compliance with the Kyoto Protocol). In the implementation of specific measures, a full quantification of the costs and benefits at a sectoral level will be undertaken.

Indicators

To assist in monitoring implementation, a robust and comprehensive set of indicators will be developed within the next year, at a sectoral and national level, under the aegis of the Climate Change Team. The primary consideration will be to measure progress towards meeting the Kyoto commitment and preparation for adopting more ambitious targets in the post-Kyoto period. Progress will be measured against the specific greenhouse gas emissions reductions targets at a sectoral level throughout this Strategy.

A range of recognised indicators is already utilised in the energy sector, and these will be expanded as necessary to provide measurements for all sectors and gases. Emphasis will also be placed on synergy with indicator series being utilised for other policy purposes. The range of indicators to be measured will include: -

- sectoral and total annual emissions of greenhouse gases;
- annual emissions reductions attributable to sectoral and to cross-sectoral policies and measures;
- energy efficiency at economy and at sectoral levels, including the degree of decoupling of economic growth from growth in energy consumption and other sources of greenhouse gas emissions;
- impacts on international competitiveness;
- cost-effectiveness and economic efficiency of measures; and
- progress towards sustainable development.

The indicators will be compared to the best international benchmark indicators for efficiency and greenhouse gas emissions performance.

Poverty Proofing

In assessing measures, full regard will be had to their contribution towards **achieving social justice and overcoming social exclusion.** Where measures are assessed as having the potential to operate against the National Anti Poverty Strategy (NAPS), compensatory approaches will be sought to offset or overcome these effects, and where appropriate, to support the overall objectives of the NAPS.

Implementing Revenue Recycling

Some of the policies identified will generate an additional stream of income, which will be recycled, through reductions in other forms of taxation, such as taxes on labour, and compensatory arrangements for sectors of society least able to bear additional costs, including through the Social Welfare Code. The full mix of policies will seek to ensure that no sector is significantly disadvantaged overall, but that all will have a greater discretion to make choices that minimise greenhouse gas emissions.

COMMUNICATING THE STRATEGY

Public awareness of climate change and public identification of the necessary action must be heightened. The Minister for the Environment and Local Government will undertake a specific campaign to address awareness, and underline the need for support for the Strategy across the economy and society. The necessary initiatives will include awareness campaigns, measures on education and information provision. These actions will be supported by the EPA, ENFO, the IEC, and Comhar. Specifically, the environmental awareness campaign, *The Environment – It's Easy to Make a Difference,* will place an emphasis on the importance of taking action now to meet the challenge of climate change, and identify a broad range of actions at the level of the individual that will contribute to reducing emissions. Further avenues to achieve behavioural change at the individual level will include further incorporation of education for sustainable development in relevant curricula; relevant utilities and sectors will also be encouraged to emphasise the underlying message on the need for climate change action in their own advertising. Comhar will develop more detailed proposals for a communications strategy as part of the Strategy implementation.

REVIEW

The Strategy will be subject to regular, biennial review, to monitor performance and assess whether additional action is necessary to meet Ireland's target. The first such review will be undertaken in 2002 by the cross-Departmental Climate Change Team in consultation with Comhar.

Particular attention will continue to be paid to the identification and implementation of further "no-regret" policies, to give maximum protection to the economy overall and to contribute towards reducing greenhouse gas concentrations in the atmosphere.

The Strategy will also be subject to review and analysis at international level, under international reporting requirements and the system of in-depth reviews carried out on country reports of activities under the Convention and Protocol, and ultimately under the Protocol compliance regime.

It will, in addition, require substantial review once commitments for the period after 2012 are negotiated.

Requirements regarding data gathering and analytical work to support this ongoing review process are set out below.

SUPPORTING MEASURES

Inventories

Inventories are prepared by the EPA, in conformity with the IPCC Guidelines, on the basis of activity data supplied by relevant Government Departments (energy balances, agriculture statistics, etc.), the census of industrial production, communications from individual emitters (e.g. industrial gases), etc. Not all activities are reported, and while the quality of the inventory is good, it is subject to ongoing improvement. For example, the national conversion factors for some activities, especially in the agriculture sector, have been developed from inadequate research. The reporting requirements under the Kyoto Protocol will be significantly more rigorous than those currently applicable under the UNFCCC, including more transparency and completeness in the inventories for the base years (1990 for all gases except the industrial gases, 1995 for these gases) and subsequent years.

Projections

Projections of greenhouse gas emissions are prepared by the EPA on the basis of projections of future activities supplied by the sources providing data for the inventories. The activity data are based on sectoral assumptions of future policy development (prepared separately in relation to energy, industrial (process), agriculture, forestry activities); it is not always clear that these assumptions are compatible with each other or compatible with macroeconomic forecasts adopted by the Department of Finance, nor are the projections always clearly developed to include expected policy developments at EU level.

An improvement in the quality of projections and their regular availability will be essential in assessing progress towards the achievement of this Strategy and identifying the need for any intensification of policies and measures or adoption of additional policies and measures.

Actions

▸ EPA capacity to meet the reporting requirements of the Kyoto Protocol will be developed, and the EPA will identify areas of priority research to be undertaken by other agencies (e.g. Teagasc). The Agencies involved will give priority to greenhouse gas emissions research. Under the RTDI and the Environment Measure of the Productive Sector Operational Programme 2000 – 2006, it is anticipated the EPA will shortly place contracts for research on emission factors; impacts of land use and land use change on carbon emission/fixation; inventory development and improvement; and impacts and indicators of climate change.

▸ The sectoral disaggregation of emissions has been identified as inadequate to meet the ongoing analytical requirements associated with sectoral contributions to limitations and reductions. Work necessary to achieve the breakdown of the underlying activity data to the level required will be undertaken as a priority, to be completed within 12 months.

▸ In order to meet the requirements of the Kyoto Protocol to make demonstrable progress by 2005, additional inventory capacity will be developed to show the "with measures"[19] and the "without measures"[20] emissions trajectories.

▸ In tandem with, and in the same timescale as the improvements in inventory provision already identified, improved projections of greenhouse gas emissions will be developed, including the quantification of "with measures" and "without measures" options, clearly indicating the quantification of the impact of the measures being

undertaken and any need for additional measures. The assumptions underlying all projections will be made explicit.

▸ The Minister for the Environment and Local Government will establish a users' group of those preparing the inventory data and those who require the output for the purposes of ongoing analysis, to assist in the development of improved inventories and projections.

---

[19] "With Measures" inventories will be those reported under the Convention and Protocol.
[20] "Without Measures" will indicate reductions below business as usual of the measures undertaken in this Strategy. Under EU proposals for the development of concrete ceilings to the amount of emissions reductions that may be achieved using the flexible mechanisms, the extent that they may be used could be related to the extent of domestic action undertaken.

Appendix 1
Science and Impacts

SCIENCE OF CLIMATE CHANGE, AND IMPACTS OF EXPECTED CHANGES

Expected Extent of Climate Change

For the IPCC mid-range emissions projection in the Second Assessment Report (1995), **global temperature** is expected to increase by 2°C by 2100 above 1990 levels, within a range of approximately 1°C to 3.5°C. The average rate of warming will probably be greater than any seen in the last 10,000 years.

Average **sea level** is expected to rise as a result of thermal expansion of the oceans and melting of glaciers and ice-sheets. The mid-range projection is about 50cm from the present to 2100, within a range 15cm to 95cm.

In the case of both temperature and sea level, these are expected to continue to increase beyond 2100 even if equilibrium is achieved in the interim in greenhouse gas concentrations.

Warmer temperatures are expected to lead to a more vigorous hydrological cycle; this translates into prospects for more severe droughts and/or floods in some places and less severe droughts and/or floods in other places. There is a possibility of an increase in precipitation intensity, suggesting a possibility for more extreme rainfall events.

There is still uncertainty related to climate change projections: - future unexpected, large and rapid changes in complex systems such as the global climate system (as have occurred in the past) are, by their nature, difficult to predict, and this implies that future climate changes may also involve "surprises". The *possible* rapid changes of particular significance to Ireland include a substantial reduction in the strength of ocean circulation (including the Gulf Stream) in the North Atlantic.

Global Implications

The IPCC has examined the impact of global climate change at a regional level. In general, it is clear that those countries that will be least in a position to meet the necessary adaptation costs are most vulnerable to the impacts of climate change and that global efforts to alleviate poverty and starvation will be greatly hampered. Vulnerability to climate change depends both on the sensitivity to climate change and the ability to adapt to these changes. A highly vulnerable system is one that is highly sensitive to modest changes in climate, where there is the potential for substantial harmful effects, and where the ability to adapt is severely constrained.

At a global level, and assuming a continuation of business as usual, without achievement of the stabilisation of greenhouse gas concentrations at levels equivalent to 550ppm to 750ppm CO_2,[21] the following broad results may be expected by the end of the 21st century.

▸ Substantial dieback of tropical forests and grasslands (including to desert) can be expected; the release into the atmosphere of the carbon stored in these ecosystems will add to overall concentrations, accelerating climate change. Temperate forests are expected to be more resilient, with an increase in vegetation biomass expected.

▸ Substantial decreases in water resources are expected in Australia, India, southern Africa, most of South America and Europe, and the Middle East, but increases in North America, central Asia, and eastern Africa.

▸ Cereal yields can be expected to increase slightly in mid and high latitudes (Canada, China, much of Europe), but the decreases in yields in Africa, India, and the Middle East are likely to more than offset these slight increases. It will be noted that the analysis that shows potential for yield increases does not fully take account of the effects of climate change in particularly vulnerable areas and the effects of extreme climate events (increases in the incidences of floods and droughts).

▸ The annual numbers of people flooded is expected to increase from approximately 15 million per annum to 90 million, mainly in southern and south eastern Asia (including India, Bangladesh, Burma, Thailand, Vietnam, Indonesia and the Philippines), but including also eastern Africa, Middle Eastern and North African coasts and western Africa. Some low-lying oceanic islands can be expected to become almost uninhabitable. Coastal wetlands are very sensitive to sea level rise, in particular rapid rise, as their location is intimately linked to present day coastlines.

▸ Global human health can be expected to be reduced through the greater spread of vector-born diseases, including up to 300 million more people at risk from malaria.

Even if stabilisation of greenhouse gas concentrations at appropriate levels can be achieved in timescales sufficient to prevent dangerous anthropogenic interference with the climate system, ongoing human-induced climate change can be expected to continue, possibly for some centuries, as certain changes lag behind changes in the atmosphere for some considerable time. Accordingly, even if emissions were rapidly to be stabilised at near-current levels, certain changes in climate may be inevitable because of the lag period: - many changes to the climate system are expected to take place as a result of the historical increase in greenhouse gas emissions over the last 2 centuries.

[21] Stabilisation of greenhouse gas emissions at twice the pre-industrial levels of CO_2 (i.e. at c. 550ppm) is envisaged in scenarios to be necessary to prevent dangerous anthropogenic intervention in the global climate system.

Appendix 2
**Gases, Inventories
and Projections**

GASES, INVENTORIES AND PROJECTIONS

Some greenhouse gases are relatively more potent at retaining solar energy in the atmosphere than others and consequently can have different effects on the climate system. Greenhouse gases also have different lifetimes in the atmosphere. To compare the different greenhouse gases, emissions are calculated on the basis of their Global Warming Potential (GWP) over a 100 year horizon, a measure of their relative heating effect in the atmosphere: -

▶ CO_2 is used as the basic unit (GWP of 1);
▶ CH_4 has a global warming effect equivalent to 21 times that of CO_2, i.e. a GWP of 21;
▶ N_2O has a GWP of 310; and
▶ the compounds included in the HFC and PFC families, and SF_6, have GWPs ranging up to 23,900.

GREENHOUSE GASES

Carbon Dioxide (CO_2)

CO_2 emissions derive largely (93.7% in 1990) from energy use, i.e. fuel combustion as an energy source for electricity generation, transport, industry, commercial and residential sectors. Emissions also arise from some industrial processes, primarily cement production, fertiliser manufacture (ammonia) and lime manufacture.

In the base year, CO_2 represented 58.7% of the basket of 6 gases. This had increased to 63.3% of net emissions by 1998, and is projected to rise to 69.6% by 2010[22]. The relative growth of CO_2 in the basket is due to the projected increase in energy use in the period 1990 to 2010 (78.8% increase in TPER), against a business as usual expectation of an 3.3% increase in emissions from agriculture (96.5% of emissions in 1990 from the sector were non-CO_2).

The sectoral sources of CO_2 in 1990, 1998 and 2010 are set out in Table A2.1 below.

There are significant increases in emissions in a number of sectors. The very large increase in transport emissions is due to a number of factors including rising vehicle numbers (almost 75% increase in private vehicles 1996 to 2010) and the increase in travel kilometres undertaken (over 100% increase expected between 1996 and 2010).[23] This is despite the 25% increase in fuel efficiency of the new vehicle fleet expected from the agreement between the EU Commission and vehicle manufacturers between 1996 and 2008.

The expected decreases in the proportion of total emissions from industry (excluding process emissions) in the period to 2010 is due to the greater use of more efficient fuels such as gas and a decrease in the energy intensity of industrial production.

Table A2.1 ('000 tonnes)

Sectoral Breakdown CO_2	1990		1998		2010	
Energy Industries	11,057	35.0%	15,047	37.6%	18,250	35.5%
Residential	6,752	21.4%	6,447	16.1%	6,470	12.6%
Transport	4,961	15.7%	8,768	21.9%	13,645	26.6%
Industry & Const	3,833	12.1%	3,917	9.8%	4,030	7.8%
Commercial/Instit	2,314	7.3%	2,775	6.9%	3,975	7.7%
Ammonia Production	989	3.1%	1,058	2.6%	1,058	2.1%
Cement	750	2.4%	1,000	2.5%	3,000	5.8%
Agri/Forestry/Fishing	660	2.1%	752	1.9%	835	1.6%
Lime Production	191	0.6%	192	0.5%	75	0.1%
Solvents	67	0.2%	71	0.2%	36	0.1%
Totals	31,575	100.0%	40,028	100.0%	51,373	100.0%

Sources: EPA (Inventories 1 March 2000; Projections 9 June 2000).

[22] All projections for 2010 in this Appendix are in accordance with Table A2.4.
[23] External Evaluator Report 26 *Update of Forecasts of Vehicle Numbers and Traffic Volumes* (DKM Economic Consultants March 1998), and compatible with *Study of Environmental Impacts of Irish Transport Growth and of Related Sustainable Policies and Measures* (Oscar Faber December 1999).

Methane (CH$_4$)

In 1990, 84.1% of all CH$_4$ emissions derived from the agriculture sector (principally enteric fermentation in ruminant animals and manure management), with 13.9% from waste (landfill gas); the remaining 2% came from energy-related emissions (energy, transport, residential and industry). Substantial reductions in CH$_4$ emissions from landfill are expected through the implementation of the waste management policies in *Changing Our Ways*.

CH$_4$ represented 23.9% of all emissions in the base year; this had decreased to 21.3% by 1998 and it is expected to decrease further to 16.2% by 2010.

The sources of CH$_4$ in 1990, 1998 and 2010 are set out in Table A2.2.

Under IPCC Guidelines, the extraction of peat and its burning for energy purposes is shown as an emission: - no provision is made in the Inventory Guidelines to offset the interruption of the CH$_4$ emissions from natural peatlands, as these emissions are non-anthropogenic. Should the IPCC Guidelines change, to allow the offsetting of CH$_4$ *not* emitted to the atmosphere from boglands that are cut for peat production, this could have a significant impact on the assessment of greenhouse gas flows from peatlands and the peat industry. However, if the Guidelines were to be changed, it is possible Ireland may have to include CH$_4$ emissions from peatlands that are managed in their natural state (e.g. Special Areas of Conservation) in the inventories and projections. Any changes in the Guidelines would be taken into account in the development of policy in relation to peat.

Nitrous Oxide (N$_2$O)

In 1990, 78.1% of all emissions of this gas derived from the agriculture sector (mostly from breakdown of nitrogenous fertilisers in the soil), with small proportions from industrial processes (production of nitric acid in the manufacture of fertiliser) and the combustion of fuels (11.4% and 10.5% respectively). Marginal decreases in emissions from 1998 levels by 2010 are expected from the amounts of nitrogenous fertilisers applied to lands; further increases from fuel combustion in energy and transport are also expected, as N$_2$O is a by-product of NOx breakdown by catalytic converters. Reductions in emissions from nitric acid production are expected.

N$_2$O represented 16.9% of all emissions in the base year; this had decreased marginally to 15.7% by 1998 and it is expected to decrease further to 12.9% by 2010.

Table A2.2 ('000 tonnes CO$_2$ equivalent)

Sectoral Breakdown CH$_4$	1990		1998		2010	
Enteric Fermentation	9,506	74.1%	10,365	76.0%	9,523	78.2%
Waste	1,780	13.9%	1,594	11.7%	1,131	9.3%
Manure Management	1,294	10.1%	1,478	10.8%	1,385	11.4%
Fugitive Emissions	127	1.0%	85	0.6%	39	0.3%
Residential	85	0.7%	55	0.4%	25	0.2%
Transport	37	0.3%	48	0.3%	76	0.6%
Commercial/Instit	4	0.0%	4	0.0%	4	0.0%
Industry & Const	3	0.0%	3	0.0%	2	0.0%
Agri/Forestry/Fishing	1	0.0%	1	0.0%	1	0.0%
Energy Industries	0	0.0%	0	0.0%	0	0.0%
Totals	12,836	100.0%	13,631	100.0%	12,185	100.0%

Sources: EPA (Inventories 1 March 2000; Projections 20 March 2000).

The sources of N_2O in 1990, 1998 and 2010, are: -

Table A2.3 ('000 tonnes CO_2 equivalent)

Sectoral Breakdown N₂0	1990		1998		2010	
Ag Soils	6,446	71.0%	7,125	70.8%	6,774	69.7%
Nitric Acid	1,036	11.4%	812	8.1%	812	8.4%
Manure Management	644	7.1%	731	7.3%	676	7.0%
Energy Industries	431	4.7%	620	6.2%	527	5.4%
Residential	182	2.0%	186	1.8%	294	3.0%
Industry & Const	117	1.3%	124	1.2%	60	0.6%
Commercial/Instit	86	1.0%	99	1.0%	73	0.8%
Transport	85	0.9%	318	3.2%	469	4.8%
Agri/Forestry/Fishing	58	0.6%	54	0.5%	34	0.3%
Totals	9,084	100.0%	10,068	100.0%	9,719	100.0%

Sources: EPA (Inventories 1 March 2000; Projections 20 March 2000).

Other Gases[24]

HFCs, PFCs and SF_6 do not occur naturally and are extremely long-lived in the atmosphere. All are manufactured for specific industrial purposes or are by-products of industrial manufacturing processes. These gases are imported to Ireland; none are manufactured here, and no industrial processes emit them as by-products. They are either incorporated into manufactured products or are fugitive emissions during manufacturing processes.

Hydrofluorocarbons (HFCs) were not in common use in 1990; they have been developed to replace CFCs, the use of which is banned under the Montreal Protocol. In Ireland, they are used for the manufacture of insulation boards, and increasingly in metered dose inhalers for sufferers from asthma and other respiratory disorders.

Perfluorocarbons (PFCs) are used in the manufacture of integrated circuits in the computer sector. Use was very low in 1990.

SF_6 is used as an insulating gas in high-tension switchgear in electricity transmission, and for some specialist functions in the manufacture of integrated circuits. This is the most potent greenhouse gas (its GWP is 23,900) but emissions are low.

It is intended to use 1995 as the base year for these gases, as provided for in the Kyoto Protocol, in line with the intention of most Parties, as data for emissions in 1990 are inadequate and emissions were insignificant until 1995.

The initial estimations are that in 1995 total emissions of all these gases together represented 0.5% of total emissions, at 256 kt CO_2 equivalent. This is expected to rise very rapidly in the period to 2010; much of the rise due to the replacement of CFCs with HFCs.

Actual and potential emissions of these gases must be identified for reporting under the Convention. Actual emissions include those gases where annual release to the atmosphere can be measured or estimated; potential emissions include gases in manufacturing or included in equipment or products, where release to the atmosphere may not occur until after a significant number of years. It has not yet been decided on what basis compliance with the Kyoto target will be determined.

Actual emissions of these gases in 2010 are expected to increase to some 672 kt CO_2 equivalent, an increase of 262%, and will represent 0.9% of the overall six gas basket.

Potential emissions, including HFCs incorporated into manufactured products, including products for export, are estimated at 1,885 kt CO_2 equivalent, or 2.6% of the basket in 2010.

[24] The inventory for these gases is a first approximation only, prepared by the Department of the Environment and Local Government; the EPA is developing full inventories and projections from 1995 as a matter of urgency.

Forest Sinks

The provisions of the Kyoto Protocol require the inclusion of certain afforestation, reforestation and deforestation activities undertaken since 1990 to be counted towards meeting the Kyoto target. The methodologies for calculating the net emissions or sink capacity are the subject of ongoing negotiations. For Ireland, however, the current afforestation programme will mean a sequestration of carbon from atmospheric CO_2, which will make a significant contribution to meeting our overall Kyoto target. In 1998, net removals of CO_2, calculated conservatively and on the basis of above-ground biomass only, pending finalisation of reporting methodologies, were 745 kt (1.2% of gross greenhouse gas emissions); by 2010, the achievement of the full national forestry programme would increase removals to an estimated 2,056 kt (2.8% of gross emissions). Even if only 50% of the projected planting is achieved, the net reduction is calculated at 1,369 kt (1.9% of gross emissions)[25].

Negotiations are also ongoing on the identification of additional categories of human activities related to agriculture soils, land use change and forestry that *may* be counted towards meeting the Kyoto target. It will be obligatory to account for these categories for the commitment periods post-2012.

Ireland is participating actively in the negotiations on the methodologies for calculating and reporting the existing Kyoto sinks and the possible additional categories of sinks, in order to ensure that Irish circumstances are taken into account to the extent possible. The Departments of Marine and Natural Resources, and Agriculture, and Food, and Rural Development are assisting the Department of the Environment and Local Government in this regard.

PROJECTIONS FOR 2010

These are based on projections of activity data supplied to the EPA from official sources and the application of internationally agreed methodologies to this data to arrive at greenhouse gas emissions.

The commitment period covers the 5 years, 2008 – 2012; projections for 2010 are taken as the mid-point of the commitment period and regarded as the average for the period.

Table A2.4 ('000 tonnes CO_2 equivalent)

	CO$_2$	CH$_4$	N$_2$O	HFC PFC SF$_6$	Total Emissions	Emissions Index	Sinks (Kyoto basis)	Net Total	Net Index
Base Year	31,575	12,836	9,085	256	53,752	100.0	0	**53,752**	100.0
1998	40,028	13,631	10,069	256	63,984	119.0	-745	**63,239**	117.6
2000	42,675	13,139	9,630	799	66,243	123.2	-991	**65,252**	121.4
2005	47,210	12,940	9,692	1,342	71,184	132.4	-1,523	**69,660**	129.6
2010 Low	51,373	12,185	9,720	672	73,950	137.6	-2,056	**71,894**	133.8
2010 High	51,373	12,185	9,720	1,885	75,163	139.8	-1,369	**73,794**	137.3

[25] Data on the carbon flows in forestry soils is incomplete; for many soils, the effect is likely to be positive, but in the case of forestry on peat soils, the overall carbon flow above and below ground may be neutral or negative.

Sources of Data

CO$_2$ Projections

For Projections to 2005: EPA, 24 August 2000, in accordance with revised 1996 IPCC Guidelines and associated software (the official basis for reporting emissions under the UNFCCC), based on ESRI energy projections (June 2000) and including non-energy sources of CO$_2$; economic growth assumptions are those in the ESRI *Medium-Term Review 1999 – 2005* (October 1999).

For 2010: EPA, 9 June 2000 from ESRI 8 June 2000.

CH$_4$ and N$_2$O Projections

EPA, March 2000, in accordance with revised 1996 IPCC Guidelines, based on data for animal numbers and agricultural activity supplied by Department of Agriculture, Food and Rural Development 3 March 1999 (average of June and December censuses for livestock numbers). 2000 projections for non-energy CH$_4$ and N$_2$O are same as for 2010.

Industrial Gases Projections

EPA, March 2000, based on incomplete 1998 survey data from Department of the Environment and Local Government. 1995 data repeated for 1998, and 2000 interpolated on straight-line basis between 1995 and 2010. Low projection for 2010 includes a proportion of HFC used by industry on the basis of the balance of production being exported (in accordance with methodologies for accounting for actual emissions). High projection for 2010 includes 100% of HFC use by industry (in accordance with methodologies for accounting for potential emissions). A 1995 base year is taken for these gases.

Sinks Projections

Department of the Environment and Local Government, in accordance with methodology used in developing EU burden sharing for counting sequestration by afforestation since 1990. This in turn based on revised dataset for forest biomass supplied by the Department of the Marine and Natural Resources to the EPA for EPA inventories and projections 18 August 1999.

High sequestration rate assumes achievement of full planting programme (25,000ha pa 1998 to 2000, 20,000ha pa post 2000, 80% conifers and 20% broadleaves). Low sequestration rate assumes 50% of programme to 2010 is achieved, in accordance with sensitivity analysis by Department of Marine and Natural Resources 6 May 1998. Carbon in forest soils, below-ground biomass, litter and forest products not counted. EPA inventory figures for sequestration reduced by 50% to allow for sigmoidal growth (i.e. lower uptake of carbon in earlier years of tree growth); maximum uptake in post-1990 forestry will be post 2012.

Range of Projections

A range is provided to reflect two possible scenarios in relation to sinks and PFC/HFC/SF$_6$ emissions. The "Low" projection assumes that: -

▸ PFC/HFC/SF$_6$ projections for 2010 are shown using the "actual" emissions approach where only amounts of substances released in Ireland are included in the net total emissions and removals;

▸ 100% of the planned forestry programme is achieved between now and 2010.

The "High" projection assumes that: -

▸ PFC/HFC/SF$_6$ emissions are allocated against the national limitation target using the "potential" emissions approach where all amounts of substances used in Ireland are included in the net total emissions and removals; most of the HFCs used are projected to be exported, and depending on the methodologies to be agreed for assigning these gases, may appear in our inventories. For the purposes of this Strategy, it is assumed that these emissions must appear in Ireland's inventory, analogous to the convention that the "embedded carbon" in the manufacture of goods requiring the use of energy or the emission of CO$_2$ from processes are shown in the inventory of the country of manufacture.

▸ 50% of the planned forestry programme is achieved between now and 2010.

These projections indicate that by the year 2010, Ireland's net greenhouse gas emissions and removals, calculated in accordance with the Kyoto Protocol, will be in the range of 71.9 – 73.8 Mt CO$_2$ equivalent, which is in the range 33.8% – 37.3% above emissions in 1990. Ireland's limitation target of 13% corresponds to a quantitative limitation target of 60.74 Mt CO$_2$ equivalent per annum for the period 2008 – 2012. Therefore, Ireland will need to achieve annual emissions savings of the order of 11.154 to 13.054 Mt CO$_2$ equivalent per annum in the commitment period.

There is a range of uncertainty in any projections, and there have been previous increases in the projections range. Accordingly, for the development of this Strategy and to prepare for post-2012 targets, it is assumed that the reduction below "business as usual" to be achieved will require to be up to 15.5 Mt CO$_2$ equivalent.

GRAPH 8	BREAKDOWN OF EMISSIONS BY GAS ON GWP BASIS, 1990, 1998 AND 2010 PROJECTIONS

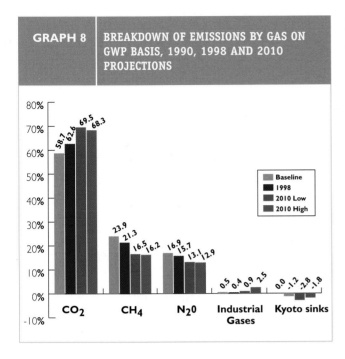

GRAPH 9	IMPACT OF STRATEGY ON ACHIEVEMENT OF KYOTO TARGET

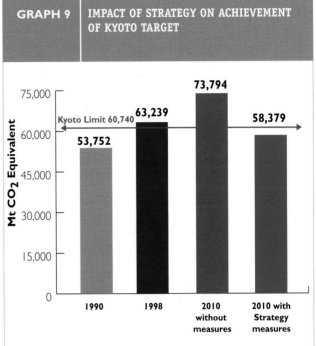

It is clear that with the expected increase in CO_2 emissions, compared to the smaller increases in CH_4 and N_2O emissions on the business as usual outlook, that CO_2 will become a larger proportion of total emissions by 2010. The secondary gases (non-CO_2), mainly from the agriculture sector, will decrease from 40.8% of the overall basket to 29.1%/29.6%. The industrial gases will account for 0.9% to 2.5% of the basket, depending on actual or potential emissions, up from a very small base (0.5% of the base year basket). **See graph 8.**

SCALE OF REDUCTIONS REQUIRED

The ERM June 1998 consultancy report has identified a quantified list of **domestic** policies and measures totalling 10 to 11 Mt CO_2 equivalent potential reductions below business as usual. Their contribution is not adequate on their own to meet the Kyoto target (assuming 10.5 Mt CO_2 equivalent reduction); accordingly the Strategy identifies adequate additional measures to meet the Kyoto target, as illustrated in **graph 9.**

The ERM report has also identified a number of additional, unquantified, policies and measures at a sectoral level which might also be adopted, in addition to cross-sectoral economic instruments (where quantification of the reduction potential was not undertaken) that may also be adopted.

The consultancy report **does not** quantify the additional reductions that will be available from common and coordinated policies and measures at EU level, nor does it quantify the reductions that may be obtained using the flexible mechanisms under the Kyoto Protocol.

SECTORAL PROJECTIONS

In developing the Strategy, it is essential to have an understanding of the sectoral sources of emissions on a business as usual basis. It is also necessary to understand the expected changes in emissions projections for each sector on foot of the Strategy. **See graphs 10-15 following.**

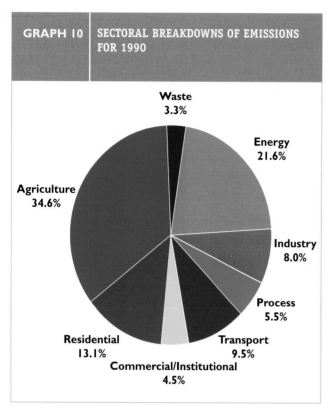

GRAPH 10 | **SECTORAL BREAKDOWNS OF EMISSIONS FOR 1990**

Waste
3.3%

Energy
21.6%

Agriculture
34.6%

Industry
8.0%

Process
5.5%

Transport
9.5%

Commercial/Institutional
4.5%

Residential
13.1%

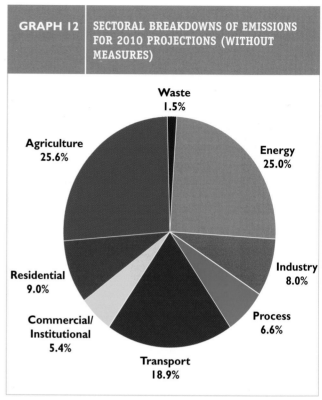

GRAPH 12 | **SECTORAL BREAKDOWNS OF EMISSIONS FOR 2010 PROJECTIONS (WITHOUT MEASURES)**

Waste
1.5%

Agriculture
25.6%

Energy
25.0%

Industry
8.0%

Residential
9.0%

Process
6.6%

Commercial/
Institutional
5.4%

Transport
18.9%

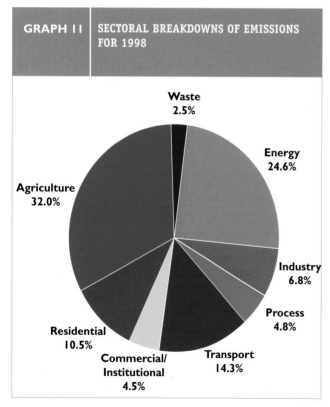

GRAPH 11 | **SECTORAL BREAKDOWNS OF EMISSIONS FOR 1998**

Waste
2.5%

Energy
24.6%

Agriculture
32.0%

Industry
6.8%

Process
4.8%

Residential
10.5%

Commercial/
Institutional
4.5%

Transport
14.3%

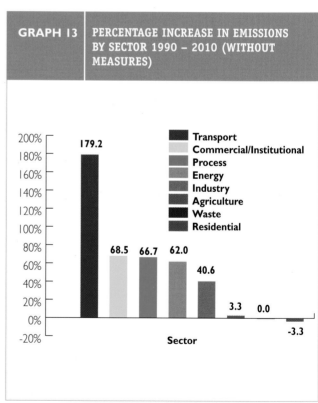

GRAPH 13 | **PERCENTAGE INCREASE IN EMISSIONS BY SECTOR 1990 – 2010 (WITHOUT MEASURES)**

- Transport
- Commercial/Institutional
- Process
- Energy
- Industry
- Agriculture
- Waste
- Residential

179.2
68.5
66.7
62.0
40.6
3.3
0.0
-3.3

Sector

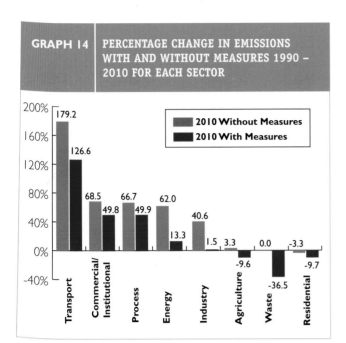

GRAPH 14 PERCENTAGE CHANGE IN EMISSIONS WITH AND WITHOUT MEASURES 1990 – 2010 FOR EACH SECTOR

Legend:
- 2010 Without Measures
- 2010 With Measures

Transport: 179.2, 126.6
Commercial/Institutional: 68.5, 49.8
Process: 66.7, 49.9
Energy: 62.0, 13.3
Industry: 40.6, 1.5
Agriculture: 3.3, -9.6
Waste: 0.0, -36.5
Residential: -3.3, -9.7

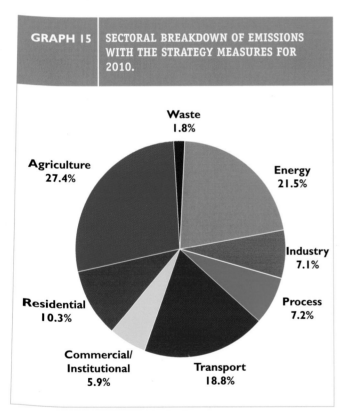

GRAPH 15 SECTORAL BREAKDOWN OF EMISSIONS WITH THE STRATEGY MEASURES FOR 2010.

Waste 1.8%
Agriculture 27.4%
Energy 21.5%
Industry 7.1%
Process 7.2%
Residential 10.3%
Transport 18.8%
Commercial/Institutional 5.9%

89